"There's nobody better than Mike Royko writing politics anywhere in the country today. About the book? It's Daley; Royko's got him to the life. And it's Chicago. Even if you've never been there you know it's Chicago. A fine job."
—Russell Baker, The New York Times

"The best book ever written about an American city by the best journalist of his time. Perhaps it will stand as the best book ever written about the American condition at this time. It comes at you from the saloons and neighborhoods, the police stations and political backrooms. It is about lies and viciousness, about the worship of cement and the hatred toward blacks, about troubling cowardice that hides behind religion and patriotism while the poor get clubbed and killed. . . . Royko's book also does more written damage to a man than perhaps any thing I have ever read. . . . I know of no place where it will not be read and quoted and kept and read again."

—Jimmy Breslin, Chicago Daily News

SIGNET and MENTOR Titles of Interest

BOSS

RICHARD J. DALEY OF CHICAGO

by Mike Royko

A SIGNET BOOK from
NEW AMERICAN LIBRARY
TIMES MIRROR

Library of Congress Catalog Card Number: 79-133585

Chapter 1 originally appeared in *Playboy* Magazine.

This is an authorized reprint of a hardcover edition published
by E. P. Dutton & Co., Inc. The hardcover edition was published simultaneously in Canada by Clarke, Irwin & Company
Limited, Toronto and Vancouver.

 SIGNET TRADEMARK REG. U.S. PAT. OFF. AND FOREIGN COUNTRIES
REGISTERED TRADEMARK——MARCA REGISTRADA
HECHO EN CHICAGO, U.S.A.

SIGNET, SIGNET CLASSICS, SIGNETTE, MENTOR AND PLUME BOOKS
are published by The New American Library, Inc.,
1301 Avenue of the Americas, New York, New York 10019

FIRST PRINTING, SEPTEMBER, 1971

11 12 13 14 15 16 17 18 19

PRINTED IN THE UNITED STATES OF AMERICA

For Dave and Rob and all the Sundays missed.

Acknowledgments

I am grateful for the help of many knowledgeable Chicagoans in putting this book together. To demonstrate my gratitude I won't name them, so they can unpack and stay in town. My thanks to Studs Terkel for talking me into it; Saul Alinsky for being around and gutsy; Leslie Q. Lubash, Howie Ziff, Stanley Koven, Nelson Algren, Al Kramer, Monsignor John Egan, Tony Scariano and Len Despres for being living reminders that everybody here wasn't born with a golden nightstick between their teeth; and Roy Fisher, a good and kind boss.

Chapter I

WILLIAM KUNSTLER: What is your name?
WITNESS: Richard Joseph Daley.
WILLIAM KUNSTLER: What is your occupation?
WITNESS: I am the mayor of the city of Chicago.

The workday begins early. Sometime after seven o'clock a black limousine glides out of the garage of the police station on the corner, moves less than a block, and stops in front of a weathered pink bungalow at 3536 South Lowe Avenue. Policeman Alphonsus Gilhooly, walking in front of the house, nods to the detective at the wheel of the limousine.

It's an unlikely house for such a car. A passing stranger might think that a rich man had come back to visit his people in the old neighborhood. It's the kind of sturdy brick house, common to Chicago, that a fireman or printer would buy. Thousands like it were put up by contractors in the 1920s and 1930s from standard blueprints in an architectural style fondly dubbed "carpenter's delight."

The outside of that pink house is deceiving. The inside is furnished in expensive, Colonial-style furniture, the basement paneled in fine wood, and two days a week a woman comes in to help with the cleaning. The shelves hold religious figurines and bric-a-brac. There are only a few volumes—the Baltimore Catechism, the Bible, a leather-bound *Profiles in Courage*, and several self-improvement books. All of the art is religious, most of it bloody with crucifixion and crosses of thorns.

Outside, another car has arrived. It moves slowly, the two detectives peering down the walkways between the houses, glancing at the drivers of the cars that travel the street, then parks somewhere behind the limousine.

At the other end of the block, a blue squad car has stopped near the corner tavern, and the policemen are watching Thirty-sixth Street, which crosses Lowe.

In the alley behind the house, a policeman sits in a car. Like Gilhooly, he has been there all night, protecting the back entrance, behind the high wooden fence that encloses the small yard.

Down the street, in another brick bungalow, Matt Danaher is getting ready for work. He runs the two thousand clerical employees in the Cook County court system, and he knows the morning routine of his neighbor. As a young protégé he once drove the car, opened the door, held the coat, got the papers. Now he is part of the ruling circle, and one of the few people in the world who can walk past the policeman and into the house, one of the people who are invited to spend an evening, sit in the basement, eat, sing, dance the Irish jig. The blue-blooded bankers from downtown aren't invited, although they would like to be, and neither are men who have been governors, senators, and ambassadors. The people who come in the evening or on Sunday are old friends from the neighborhood, the relatives, people who take their coats off when they walk in the door, and loosen their ties.

Danaher is one of them, and his relationship to the owner of the house is so close that he has served as an emotional whipping boy, so close that he can yell back and slam the door when he leaves.

They're getting up for work in the little houses and flats all across the old neighborhood known as Bridgeport, and thanks to the man for whom the limousine waits, about two thousand of the forty thousand Bridgeport people are going to jobs in City Hall, the County Building, the courts,

ward offices, police and fire stations. It's a political neighborhood, with political jobs, and the people can use them.
It ranks very low among the city and suburban communities in education. Those who don't have government jobs
work hard for their money, and it isn't much. Bridgeport
ranks low in income, too.

It's a suspicious neighborhood, a blend of Irish, Lithuanian, Italian, Polish, German, and all white. In the bars,
heads turn when a stranger comes in. Blacks pass through
in cars, but are unwise to travel by on foot. When a black
college student moved into a flat on Lowe Avenue in 1964,
only a block north of the pink bungalow, there was a riot
and he had to leave.

Well before eight o'clock, the door of the bungalow
opens and a short, stout man steps out. His walk is brisk
and bouncy. A nod and smile to Patrolman Gilhooly and
he's in the limousine. It pulls out from the curb and the
"tail car" with the two detectives trails it, hanging back
to prevent the limousine from being followed.

It's a short drive to work. The house is about four
miles southwest of the Loop, the downtown business
district, within the problem area known as the "inner
city." If the limousine went east, to Lake Shore Drive,
it would go through part of the black ghetto. If it went
straight north, it would enter a decaying neighborhood in
transition from white to Latin and black. It turns toward
an expressway entrance only a few blocks away.

The two cars take the Dan Ryan Expressway, twelve
lanes at its widest point, with a rapid-transit train track
down the center. It stretches from the Loop, past the old
South Side ghetto, past the giant beehive public housing
with its swarming children, furious street gangs, and
weary welfare mothers.

He built that expressway, and he named it after Dan
Ryan, another big South Side politician, who was named
after his father, a big South Side politician.

The limousine crosses another expressway, this one
cutting through the big, smokey, industrial belt, southwest
toward white backlash country, where five years ago Dr.
Martin Luther King was hit in the head with a brick when
he led marchers into the neighborhood for the cause of

open housing—which exists only on a few pages of the city's ordinance.

He built that expressway, too, and named it after Adlai Stevenson, whom he helped build into a presidential candidate, and whom he dropped when it was time.

The limousine passes an exit that leads to the Circle Campus, the city's branch of the University of Illinois, acres of modern concrete buildings that comprise one of the biggest city campuses in the country. It wasn't easy to build because thousands of families in the city's oldest Italian neighborhood had to be uprooted and their homes and churches torn down. They cried that they were betrayed because they had been promised they would stay. But he built it.

Another mile or so and the limousine crosses another expressway that goes straight west, through the worst of the ghetto slums, where the biggest riots and fires were ignited, for which the outraged and outrageous "shoot to kill" order was issued. Straight west, past the house where the Black Panthers were killed, some in their beds, by the predawn police raiders.

He opened that expressway and named it after Dwight D. Eisenhower, making it the city's only Republican expressway.

As the limousine nears the Loop, the Dan Ryan blends into still another expressway. This one goes through the Puerto Rican ghetto and the remnants of the old Polish neighborhood, where the old people remain while their children move away, then into the middle class far Northwest Side, where Dr. King's marchers walked through a shower of bottles, bricks and spit. It ends at O'Hare Airport, the nation's busiest jet handler.

He built that expressway, too, and he named it after John F. Kennedy, whom he helped elect president, and he built most of the airport and opened it, although he still calls it "O'Hara."

During the ride he reads the two morning papers, the *Chicago Sun-Times* and the *Chicago Tribune,* always waiting on the back seat. He's a fast but thorough reader and he concentrates on news about the city. He is in the papers somewhere every day, if not by name—and the omission is rare—at least by deed. The papers like him.

If something has gone well, he'll be praised in an editorial. If something has gone badly, one of his subordinates will be criticized in an editorial. During the 1968 Democratic Convention, when their reporters were being bloodied, one of the more scathing newspaper editorials was directed at a lowly Police Department public relations man.

He, too, was criticized, but a week after the convention ended, his official version of what had happened on Chicago's streets was printed, its distortions and flat lies unchallenged. He dislikes reporters and writers, but gets on well with editors and publishers, a trait usually found in Republicans rather than Democrats. If he feels that he has been criticized unfairly, and he considers most criticism unfair, he doesn't hesitate to pick up a phone and complain to an editor. All four papers endorsed him for his fourth term—even the *Tribune,* the voice of Middle West Republicanism—but in general, he views the papers as his enemy. The reporters, specifically. They want to know things that are none of their business, because they are little men. Editors, at least, have power, but he doesn't understand why they let reporters exercise it.

The limousine leaves the expressway and enters the Loop, stopping in front of St. Peter's, a downtown church. When the bodyguards have parked and walked to his car, he gets out and enters the church. This is an important part of his day. Since childhood he has attended daily mass, as his mother did before him. On Sundays and some work days, he'll go to his own church, the Church of the Nativity, just around the corner from his home. That's where he was baptized, married, and the place from which his parents were buried. Before Easter, his wife will join the other neighborhood ladies for the traditional scrubbing of the church floors. Regardless of what he may do in the afternoon, and to whom, he will always pray in the morning.

After mass, it's a few steps to the side door of Maxim's, a glass and plastic coffee shop, where, in the event he comes in, a table is set up in the privacy of the rear. It is not to be confused with Chicago's other Maxim's which serves haute cuisine, has a discotheque, and enjoys a social-register clientele. He won't go to those kinds of places. He doesn't like them and people might think he was putting on airs. He eats at home most of the time, and for dinner out there are sedate private clubs with a table in a quiet corner.

He leaves a dollar for his coffee and roll and marches with his bodyguards toward City Hall—"the Hall," as it is called locally, as in "I got a job in the Hall," or "See my brother in the Hall and he'll fix it for you," or "Do you know anybody in the Hall who can take care of this?"

He glances at the new Civic Center, a tower of russet steel and glass, fronted by a gracious plaza with a fountain and a genuine Picasso-designed metalwork sculpture almost fifty feet high.

He put it all there, the Civic Center, the plaza, the Picasso. And the judges and county officials who work in the Civic Center, he put most of them there, too.

Wherever he looks as he marches, there are new skyscrapers up or going up. The city has become an architect's delight, except when the architects see the great Louis Sullivan's landmark buildings being ripped down for parking garages or allowed to degenerate into slums.

None of the new buildings were there before. His leadership put them there, his confidence, his energy. Everybody says so. If he kept walking north a couple more blocks, he'd see the twin towers of Marina City, the striking tubular downtown apartment buildings, a self-contained city with bars and restaurants, ice rinks, shops and clubs, and balconies on every apartment for sitting out in the smog.

His good friend Charlie Swibel built it, with financing from the Janitors' Union, run by his good friend William McFetridge. For Charlie Swibel, building the apartment towers was coming a long way from being a flophouse and slum operator. Now some of his friend Charlie's flophouses are going to be torn down, and the area west of the Loop redeveloped for office buildings and such. And his friend Charlie will do that, too. Let people wonder why out-of-town investors let Charlie in for a big piece of the new project, without Charlie having to put up any money or take any risk. Let people ask why the city, after acquiring the land under urban renewal powers, rushed through approval of Charlie's bid. Let them ask if there's a conflict of interest because Charlie is also the head of the city's public housing agency, which makes him a city official. Let them ask. What trees do they plant? What buildings do they put up?

Head high, shoulders back, he strides with his body-guards at the pace of an infantry forced march. The morning walk used to be much longer than two blocks. In the quiet of the 1950s, the limousine dropped him near the Art Institute on Michigan Avenue, and he'd walk a mile and a half on Michigan Avenue, the city's jeweled thoroughfare, grinning at the morning crowds that bustled past the shops and hotels, along the edge of Grant Park. That ritual ended in the sixties, when people began walking and marching for something more than pleasure, and a man couldn't be sure who he'd meet on the street.

He rounds the corner and a bodyguard moves ahead to hold open the door. An elderly man is walking slowly and painfully close to the wall, using it as support. His name is Al, and he is a lawyer. Years ago he was just a ward boss's nod away from becoming a judge. He had worked hard for the party and had earned the black robe, and he was even a pretty good lawyer. But the ward boss died on him, and judgeships can't be left in wills. Now his health was bad and Al had an undemanding job in county government.

He spots Al, calls out his name, and rushes over and gives him a two-handed handshake, the maximum in City Hall affection. He has seen Al twice in ten years, but he quickly recalls all of his problems, his work, and a memory they shared. He likes old people and keeps them in key jobs and reslates them for office when they can barely walk, or even when they can't. Like the marriage vows, the pact between jobholder and party ends only in either's death, so long as the jobholder loves, honors, and obeys the party. Later that day, Al will write an eloquent letter in praise of his old friend to a paper, which will print it.

The bodyguard is still holding the door and he goes in at full stride. He never enters a room tentatively—always explosively and with a sense of purpose and direction, especially when the building is City Hall.

Actually, there are two identical buildings—City Hall and Cook County Building. At the turn of the century, the County Building was erected on half a city block, and shortly thereafter City Hall was put up. Although identical, City Hall cost substantially more. Chicago history is full of such oddities. Flip open any page and somebody is making a buck.

Although the main lobby and upstairs corridors extend through both buildings, he never goes through the County Building. That's a political courtesy, because the County Building is the domain of another politician, the president of the Cook County Board, known as "the mayor of Cook County," and, in theory, second only to him in power. But later in the day, the president of Cook County will call and ask how his domain should be run.

The elevator operators know his habits and are holding back the door of a car. The elevators are automated, but many operators remain on the job, standing in the lobby pointing at open cars and saying, "Next." Automation is fine, but how many votes can an automatic elevator deliver?

He gets off at the fifth floor, where his offices are. That's why he's known as "the Man on Five." He is also known as "duh mare" and "hizzoner" and "duh leader."

He marches past the main entrance to his outer offices, where people are already waiting, hoping to see him. They must be cleared first by policemen, then by three secretaries. He doesn't use the main entrance because the people would jump up, clutch at his hands, and overexcite themselves. He was striding through the building one day when a little man sprung past the bodyguards and kissed his hand.

Down the corridor, a bodyguard has opened a private door, leading directly to his three-room office complex. He almost always uses the side door.

The bodyguards quickly check his office then file into a smaller adjoining room, filled with keepsakes from presidents and his trip to Ireland. They use the room as a lounge, while studying his schedule, planning the routes and waiting. Another room is where he takes important phone calls when he has someone with him. Calls from President Kennedy and President Johnson were put through to that room.

Somewhere in the building, phone experts have checked

his lines for taps. The limousine has been parked on LaSalle Street, outside the Hall's main entrance, and the tail car has moved into place. His key people are already in their offices, always on time or early, because he may call as soon as he arrives. And at 9 A.M. he, Richard Joseph Daley, is in his office and behind the big gleaming mahogany desk, in a high-backed dark green leather chair, ready to start another day of doing what the experts say is no longer possible—running a big American city. But as he, Daley, has often said to confidantes, "What in hell do the experts know?" He's been running a big American city for fifteen of the toughest years American cities have ever seen. He, Daley, has been running it as long or longer than any of the other famous mayors—Curley of Boston, LaGuardia of New York, Kelly of Chicago—ran theirs, and unless his health goes, or his wife says no, he, Daley, will be running it for another four years. Twenty is a nice, round figure. They give soldiers pensions after twenty years, and some companies give wristwatches. He'll settle for something simple, like maybe another jet airport built on a man-made island in the lake, and named after him, and maybe a statue outside the Civic Center, with a simple inscription, "The greatest mayor in the history of the world." And they might seal off his office as a shrine.

It's a business office. Like the man, the surroundings have no distracting frills. He wears excellently tailored business suits, buying six a year from the best shop on Michigan Avenue. The shirt is always radiant white, the tie conservative. Because his shoulders are narrow, he never works in his shirt sleeves, and is seldom seen publicly in casual clothes. The businesslike appearance carries through the office. The carpets, furniture, and walls are in muted shades of tan and green. The only color is provided by the flags of the United States and the city of Chicago, and a color photograph of his family. When a prominent cultural leader offered to donate some paintings for the office, an aide said, "Please, no, he can't accept them. People would think he's going high-hat."

The desk, with a green leather inset, is always clear of papers. He is an orderly man. Besides, he doesn't like to put things on paper, preferring the telephone. Historians will look in vain for a revealing memo, an angry note. He stores his information in his brain and has an amazing recall of detail.

The office is a place to work. And the work begins immediately. The first call will be to his secretary, checking the waiting visitors and asking that his press secretary be summoned, so he can let him know if he wants to talk to the press that morning. He holds more press conferences than any major public official in the country—at least two, and usually three, a week. In the beginning, they were often relaxed, casual, friendly and easy, with the reporters coming into his office, getting the q's and a's out of the way, and swapping fish stories and a few jokes, but always clean jokes because he walks away from the dirty ones. But with television, the press conferences became formal. They moved to a conference room, and became less friendly as the times became less friendly. He works at self-control, but it is impossible not to blow up and begin ranting. Reporters are like experts. What do they know?

If he is going to see them, Earl Bush, the press aide, will brief him on likely questions. The veteran City Hall reporters are not hostile, since they have to live with him, but the TV personalities sometimes ask questions that are calculated to cause a purple face and a fit of shouting rather than evoke information. He knows it, but sometimes it is hard not to get purple and shout.

If he doesn't feel like bothering, he'll just tell Bush, "To hell with them," and go on to other work. Bush never argues. He's been there since the beginning, a hungry journalist, operating a struggling neighborhood newspaper news service, who had a hunch that the quiet man running the county clerk's office was going to go somewhere. On the day after the first mayoralty election, Daley threw three hundred-dollar bills in his rumpled lap and said, "Get yourself some decent-looking clothes." Bush has since slept a night in the White House.

After Bush will come someone like Deputy Mayor David Stahl, one of the young administrators the old politicians call "the whiz kids." Like the other "whiz kids," Stahl is serious, well educated, obedient, ambitious, and keeps his sense of humor out of sight. He was hired for these qualities and also because his father-in-law is a real estate expert and a close friend.

On a day when the City Council is meeting, Ald. Thomas Keane will slip in the side door to brief him on the agenda. Keane is considered to be second in party power, but it is a distant second. Keane wanted to be in front, but he was distracted by a craving for personal wealth. You can't do both if the man you're chasing is concentrating only on power. Now Keane is rich, but too old to ever be the successor.

If there is a council meeting, everybody marches downstairs at a few mintues before ten. Bush and the department heads and personal aides form a proud parade. The meeting begins when the seat of the mayor's pants touches the council president's chair, placed beneath the great seal of the city of Chicago and above the heads of the aldermen, who sit in a semi-bowl auditorium.

It is his council, and in all the years it has never once defied him as a body. Keane manages it for him, and most of its members do what they are told. In other eras, the aldermen ran the city and plundered it. In his boyhood they were so constantly on the prowl that they were known as "the Gray Wolves." His council is known as "the Rubber Stamp."

He looks down at them, bestowing a nod or a benign smile on a few favorites, and they smile back gratefully. He seldom nods or smiles at the small minority of white and black independents. The independents anger him more than the Republicans do, because they accuse him of racism, fascism, and of being a dictator. The Republicans bluster about loafing payrollers, crumbling gutters, inflated budgets—traditional, comfortable accusations that don't stir the blood.

That is what Keane is for. When the minority goes on the attack, Keane himself, or one of the administration aldermen he has groomed for the purpose, will rise and answer the criticism by shouting that the critic is a fool, a hypocrite, ignorant, and misguided. Until his death, one alderman could be expected to leap to his feet at every meeting and cry, "God bless our mayor, the greatest mayor in the world."

But sometimes Keane and his trained orators can't

shout down the minority, so Daley has to do it himself. If provoked, he'll break into a rambling, ranting speech, waving his arms, shaking his fists, defending his judgment, defending his administration, always with the familiar "It is easy to criticize . . . to find fault . . . but where are your programs . . . where are your ideas . . ."

If that doesn't shut off the critics, he will declare them to be out of order, threaten to have the sergeant at arms force them into their seats, and invoke *Robert's Rules of Orders,* which, in the heat of debate, he once described as "the greatest book ever written."

All else failing, he will look toward a glass booth above the spectator's balcony and make a gesture known only to the man in the booth who operates the sound system that controls the microphones on each alderman's desk. The man in the booth will touch a switch and the offending critic's microphone will go dead and stay dead until he sinks into his chair and closes his mouth.

The meetings are seldom peaceful and orderly. The slightest criticism touches off shrill rebuttal, leading to louder criticism and finally an embarrassingly wild and vicious free-for-all. It can't be true, because Daley is a man who speaks highly of law and order, but sometimes it appears that he enjoys the chaos, and he seldom moves to end it until it has raged out of control.

Every word of criticism must be answered, every complaint must be disproved, every insult must be returned in kind. He doesn't take anything from anybody. While Daley was mediating negotiations between white trade unions and black groups who wanted the unions to accept blacks, a young militant angrily rejected one of his suggestions and concluded, "Up your ass!" Daley leaped to his feet and answered, "And up yours too." Would John Lindsay have become so involved?

Independent aldermen have been known to come up with a good idea, such as providing food for the city's hungry, or starting day-care centers for children of ghetto women who want to work; Daley will acknowledge it, but in his own way. He'll let Keane appropriate the idea and rewrite and resubmit it as an administration measure. That way, the independent has the satisfaction of seeing his idea reach fruition and the administration has more glory.

But most of the independents' proposals are sent to a special subcommittee that exists solely to allow their unwelcome ideas to die.

The council meetings seldom last beyond the lunch hour. Aldermen have much to do. Many are lawyers and have thriving practices, because Chicagoans know that a dumb lawyer who is an alderman can often perform greater legal miracles than a smart lawyer who isn't.

Keane will go to a hotel dining room near City Hall, where at a large round table in a corner, he lunches each day with a clique of high-rise real estate developers, financiers, and political cronies. The things they plan and share will shape the future of the city, as well as the future of their heirs.

Daley has no such luncheon circle, and he eats only with old and close friends or one of his sons. Most afternoons, he darts across the street to the Sherman House hotel and his office in the Democratic headquarters, where as party chairman he will work on purely political business: somebody pleading to be slated for an office or advanced to a judgeship, a dispute between ward bosses over patronage jobs. He tries to separate political work from his duties as mayor, but nobody has ever been able to see where one ends and the other begins.

Lunch will be sent up and he might be joined by someone like Raymond Simon, the Bridgeport-born son of an old friend. Daley put him in the city legal department when he was fresh out of law school, and in a few years he was placed in charge, one of the highest legal jobs in the country. Now Simon has taken on an even bigger job: he resigned and went into private practice with Daley's oldest son, Richard Michael, not long out of law school. The name Daley and Simon on the office door possesses magic that has the big clients almost waiting in line. Daley's next oldest son, Michael, has gone into practice with a former law partner of the mayor, and has a surprisingly prosperous practice for so young and inexperienced an attorney. Daley filled Simon's place in his cabinet with another bright young lawyer, the mayor's first cousin.

When there is time, Daley is driven to the private Lake Shore Club for lunch, a swim, or a steam bath. Like most of the better private clubs in the fine buildings along the lake front, the Lake Shore Club accepts Jews and blacks. But you have to sit there all day to be sure of seeing one.

It's a pleasant drive to the club. Going north on Michigan Avenue, he passes the John Hancock Building, second in size only to the Empire State, and twice as high as anything near it. It was built during Daley's fourth term, despite cries of those who said it would bring intolerable traffic congestion to the gracious streets that can't handle it and lead to other oversized buildings that would destroy the unique flavor of the North Michigan Avenue district. It's happening, too, but the Hancock is another tall monument to his leadership.

From Michigan Avenue, he goes onto Lake Shore Drive, with the lake and beaches on the right, which were there when he started, and ahead the great wall of high-rise buildings beginning on the left, which wasn't. Dozens of them, hundreds, stretching mile after mile, all the way to the city limits, and almost all constructed during his administration, providing city living for the upper middle class, and billions in profits for the real estate developers. They are his administration's solution to keeping people in the city.

Behind the high-rises are the crumbling, crowded buildings where the lower-income people live. No answer has been found to their housing problems because the real estate people say there's not enough profit in building homes for them. And beyond them are the middle-income people, who can't make it to the high-rises and can't stay where they are because the schools are inadequate, the poor are pushing toward them, and nothing is being done about their problems, so they move to the suburbs. When their children grow up and they retire, maybe then they can move to a lake front high-rise.

By two o'clock he's back behind his desk and working. One of his visitors will be a city official unique to Chicago city government: the director of patronage. He brings a list of all new city employees for the day. The list isn't limited to the key employees, the professional people. All new employees are there—down to the window washer, the ditch digger, the garbage collector. After each person's name will be an extract of his background, the job, and most important, his political sponsor. Nobody goes to work for the city, and that includes governmental bodies that are not directly under the mayor, without Daley's knowing about it. He must see every name because the person becomes more than an employee: he joins the political Machine, part of the army numbering in the thousands who will help win elections. They damn well better, or they won't keep their jobs.

He scans the list for anything unusual. A new employee might be related to somebody special, an important businessman, an old political family. That will be noted. He might have been fired by another city office in a scandal. That won't keep him from being put to work somewhere else. Some bad ones have worked for half the governmental offices in the city. There might be a police record, which prompts a call to the political sponsor for an explanation. "He's clean now." "Are you sure?" "Of course, it was just a youthful mistake." "Three times?" "Give him a break, his uncle is my best precinct captain." "Okay, a break, but keep your eye on him." As he has said so often, when the subject of ex-cons on the city payroll comes up, "Are we to deny these men honest employment in a free society . . . are we to deprive them of the right to work . . . to become rehabilitated . . ." He will forgive anything short of Republicanism.

The afternoon work moves with never a minute wasted. The engineers and planners come with their reports on public works projects. Something is always being built, concrete being poured, steel being riveted, contractors being enriched.

"When will it be completed?" he asks.

"Early February."

"It would be a good thing for the people if it could be completed by the end of October."

The engineers say it can be done, but it will mean putting on extra shifts, night work, overtime pay, a much higher cost than was planned.

"It would be a good thing for the people if it could be completed by the end of October."

Of course it would be a good thing for the people. It would also be a good thing for the Democratic candidates who are seeking election in early November to go out and cut a ribbon for a new expressway or a water filtration plant or, if nothing else is handy, another wing at the O'Hare terminal. What ribbons do their opponents cut?

The engineers and planners understand, and they set about getting it finished by October.

On a good afternoon, there will be no neighborhood organizations to see him, because if they get to Daley, it means they have been up the ladder of government and nobody has been able to solve their problem. And that usually means a conflict between the people and somebody else, such as a politician or a business, whom his aides don't want to ruffle. There are many things his department heads can't do. They can't cross swords with ward bosses or politically heavy businessmen. They can't make important decisions. Some can't even make petty decisions. He runs City Hall like a small family business and keeps everybody on a short rein. They do only that which they know is safe and that which he tells them to do. So many things that should logically be solved several rungs below finally come to him.

Because of this, he has many requests from neighborhood people. And when a group is admitted to his office, most of them nervous and wide-eyed, he knows who they are, their leaders, their strength in the community. They have already been checked out by somebody. He must know everything. He doesn't like to be surprised. Just as he knows the name of every new worker, he must know what is going on in the various city offices. If the head of the office doesn't tell him, he has somebody there who will. In the office of other elected officials, he has trusted persons who will keep him informed. Out in the neighborhoods his precinct captains are reporting to the ward committeemen, and they in turn are reporting to him.

His police department's intelligence-gathering division gets bigger and bigger, its network of infiltrators, informers, and spies creating massive files on dissenters, street gangs, political enemies, newsmen, radicals, liberals, and anybody else who might be working against him. If one of his aides or handpicked officeholders is shacking up with a woman, he will know it. And if that man is married and a Catholic, his political career will wither and die. That is the greatest sin of all. You can make money under the table and move ahead, but you are forbidden to make secretaries under the sheets. He has dumped several party members for violating his personal moral standards. If something is leaked to the press, the bigmouth will be tracked down and punished. Scandals aren't public scandals if you get there before your enemies do.

So when the people come in, he knows what they want and whether it is possible. Not that it means they will get it. That often depends on how they act.

He will come out from behind his desk all smiles and handshakes and charm. Then he returns to his chair and sits very straight, hands folded on his immaculate desk, serious and attentive. To one side will be somebody from the appropriate city department.

Now it's up to the group. If they are respectful, he will express sympathy, ask encouraging questions, and finally tell them that everything possible will be done. And after they leave, he may say, "Take care of it." With that command, the royal seal, anything is possible, anybody's toes can be stepped on.

But if they are pushy, antagonistic, demanding instead of imploring, or bold enough to be critical of him, to tell him how he should do his job, to blame him for their problem, he will rub his hands together, harder and harder. In a long, difficult meeting, his hands will get raw. His voice gets lower, softer, and the corners of his mouth will turn down. At this point, those who know him will back off. They know what's next. But the unfamiliar, the militant, will mistake his lowered voice and nervousness for weakness. Then he'll blow, and it comes in a frantic roar:

"I want *you* to tell *me* what to do. *You* come up with the answers. *You* come up with the program. Are we perfect? Are *you* perfect? We all make mistakes. We all have faults. It's easy to criticize. It's easy to find fault. But *you* tell me what to do. This problem is all over the city. We didn't create these problems. We don't want them. But we are doing what we can. *You* tell me how to solve them. *You* give me a program." All of which leaves the petitioners dumb, since most people don't walk around with urban programs in their pockets. It can also leave them right back where they started.

They leave and the favor seekers come in. Half of the

people he sees want a favor. They plead for promotions, something for their sons, a chance to do some business with the city, to get somebody in City Hall off their backs, a chance to return from political exile, a boon. They won't get an answer right there and then. It will be considered and he'll let them know. Later, sometimes much later, when he has considered the alternatives and the benefits, word will get back to them. Yes or no. Success or failure. Life or death.

Some jobseekers come directly to him. Complete outsiders, meaning those with no family or political connections, will be sent to see their ward committeemen. That is protocol, and that is what he did to the tall young black man who came to see him a few years ago, bearing a letter from the governor of North Carolina, who wrote that the young black man was a rising political prospect in his state. Daley told him to see his ward committeeman, and if he did some precinct work, rang doorbells, hustled up some votes, there might be a government job for him. Maybe something like taking coins in a tollway booth. The Rev. Jesse Jackson, now the city's leading black civil rights leader, still hasn't stopped smarting over that.

Others come asking him to resolve a problem. He is the city's leading labor mediator and has prevented the kind of strikes that have crippled New York. His father was a union man, and he comes from a union neighborhood, and many of the union leaders were his boyhood friends. He knows what they want. And if it is in the city's treasury, they will get it. If it isn't there, he'll promise to find it. He has ended a teachers' strike by promising that the state legislature would find funds for them, which surprised the Republicans in Springfield, as well as put them on the spot. He is an effective mediator with the management side of labor disputes, because they respect his judgment, and because there are few industries that do not need some favors from City Hall.

There are disputes he won't bother with, such as that between two ranking party members, both lawyers, each retained by a rival business interest in a zoning dispute. That was the kind of situation that can drive judges, city agencies, and functionaries berserk. He angrily wiped his hands of the matter, bawled the lawyers out for creating the mess, and let them take their chances on a fair decision. There are so many clients, peace should exist among friends.

The afternoon is almost gone, but they still keep coming in the front door and those he summons through the side. The phone keeps ringing, bringing reports from his legislators in Springfield, his congressmen in Washington, and prominent businessmen, some of whom may waste a minute of his time for the status of telling dinner guests, "I mentioned that to Dick and he likes the idea . . ."

Finally the scheduled appointments have been cleared, the unscheduled hopefuls told to come back again, and a few late calls made to his closest aides. It's six o'clock, but he is still going, as if reluctant to stop. The workdays have grown longer over the years, the vacations shorter. There is less visible joy in it all, but he works harder now than ever before. Some of his friends say he isn't comfortable anywhere but in the office on five.

The bodyguards check the corridor and he heads downstairs to the limousine. Most of the people in the Hall have left, and the mop crews are going to work, but always on the sidewalk outside will be the old hangers-on, waiting to shout a greeting, to get a nod or a smile in return.

On the way out, Bush hands him a speech. That's for the next stop, a banquet of civic leaders, or a professional group, or an important convention. The hotel grand ballroom is a couple of minutes away and he'll speed-read the speech just once on the way, a habit that contributes to his strange style of public speaking, with the emphasis often on the wrong words, the sentences overlapping, and the words tumbling over each other. Regardless of where he goes, the speech will be heavy in boosterism, full of optimism for the future, pride in the city, a reminder of what he has done. Even in the most important of gatherings, people will seek out his handshake, his recognition. A long time ago, when they opposed him, he put out the hand and moved the few steps to them. Now they come to him. He arrives after dinner, in time to be introduced, speak, and get back to the car.

The afternoon papers are on the back seat and he reads them until the limousine stops in front of a funeral home. Wakes are still part of political courtesy and his culture.

Since he started in politics, he's been to a thousand of them. On the way up, the slightest connection with the deceased or his family was enough reason to attend a wake. Now he goes to fewer, and only to those involving friends, neighbors. His sons fill in for him at others. Most likely, he'll go to a wake on the South Side, because that's where most of his old friends are from. The funeral home might be McInerney's, which has matchbooks that bear a poem beginning, "Bring out the lace curtains and call McInerney, I'm nearing the end of life's pleasant journey." Or John Egan's, one of the biggest, owned by his high school pal and one of the last of the successful undertaker-politicians. The undertaker-politicians and the saloon keeper–politicians have given way to lawyer-politicians, who are no better, and they don't even buy you a drink or offer a prayer.

He knows how to act at a wake, greeting the immediate family, saying the proper things, offering his regrets, somberly and with dignity. His arrival is as big an event as the other fellow's departure. Before leaving, he will kneel at the casket, an honor afforded few of the living, and sign the visitor's book. A flurry of handshakes and he is back in the car.

It's late when the limousine turns toward Bridgeport. His neighbors are already home watching TV or at the Pump Tavern having a beer, talking baseball, race or politics. His wife Eleanor, "Sis" as he calls her, knows his schedule and will be making supper. Something boiled, meat and potatoes, home-baked bread. She makes six loaves a week. His mother always made bread. And maybe ice cream for dessert. He likes ice cream. There's an old ice cream parlor in the neighborhood, and sometimes he goes there for a sundae, as he did when he was a boy.

The limousine passes Comiskey Park, where his beloved Sox play ball. He goes to Wrigley Field, too, but only to be seen. The Sox are his team. He can walk to the ball park from the house. At least he used to be able to walk there. Today it's not the same. A person can't walk anywhere. Maybe someday he'll build a big superstadium for all the teams, better than any other city's. Maybe on the Lake Front. Let the conservationists moan. It will be good for business, drawing conventioneers from hotels, and

near an expressway so people in the suburbs can drive
in. With lots of parking space for them, and bright lights
so they can walk. Some day, if there's time, he might just
build it.

Across Halsted Street, then a turn down Lowe Avenue,
into the glow of the brightest street lights of any city in
the country. The streets were so dark before, a person
couldn't see who was there. Now all the streets have
lights so bright that some people have to lower their shades
at night. He turned on all those lights, he built them. Now
he can see a block ahead from his car, to where the policeman is guarding the front of his home.

He tells the driver that tomorrow will require an even
earlier start. He must catch a flight to Washington to tell
a committee that the cities need more money. There are
so many things that must be built, so many more people to
be hired. But he'll be back the same day, in the afternoon,
with enough time to maybe stop at the Hall. There's always something to do there. Things have to be done. If
he doesn't do them, who will?

Chapter II

KUNSTLER: Mayor Daley, do you know a federal
  judge by the name of Judge Lynch?
WITNESS: Do I know him?
KUNSTLER: Yes.
WITNESS: . . . We have been boyhood friends all our
  lives.

He grew up a small-town boy, which used to be possible
even in the big city. Not anymore, because of the car, the
shifting society, and the suburban sprawl. But Chicago,
until as late as the 1950s, was a place where people stayed
put for a while, creating tightly knit neighborhoods, as
small-townish as any village in the wheat fields.

The neighborhood-towns were part of larger ethnic
states. To the north of the Loop was Germany. To the
northwest Poland. To the west were Italy and Israel.
To the southwest were Bohemia and Lithuania. And to
the south was Ireland.

It wasn't perfectly defined because the borders shifted
as newcomers moved in on the old settlers, sending them
fleeing in terror and disgust. Here and there were outlying
colonies, with Poles also on the South Side, and Irish up
north.

But you could always tell, even with your eyes closed,

which state you were in by the odors of the food stores and the open kitchen windows, the sound of the foreign or familiar language, and by whether a stranger hit you in the head with a rock.

In every neighborhood could be found all the ingredients of the small town: the local tavern, the funeral parlor, the bakery, the vegetable store, the butcher shop, the drugstore, the neighborhood drunk, the neighborhood trollop, the neighborhood idiot, the neighborhood war hero, the neighborhood police station, the neighborhood team, the neighborhood sports star, the ball field, the barber shop, the pool hall, the clubs, and the main street.

Every neighborhood had a main street for shopping and public transportation. The city is laid out with a main street every half mile, residential streets between. But even better than in a small town, a neighborhood person didn't have to go over to the main street to get essentials, such as food and drink. On the side streets were taverns and little grocery stores. To buy new underwear, though, you had to go to Main Street.

With everything right there, why go anywhere else? If you went somewhere else, you couldn't get credit, you'd have to waste a nickel on the streetcar, and when you finally got there, they might not speak the language.

Some people had to leave the neighborhood to work, but many didn't, because the houses were interlaced with industry.

On Sunday, people might ride a streetcar to visit a relative, but they usually remained within the ethnic state, unless there had been an unfortunate marriage in the family.

The borders of neighborhoods were the main streets, railroad tracks, branches of the Chicago River, branches of the branches, strips of industry, parks, and anything else that could be glared across.

The ethnic states got along just about as pleasantly as did the nations of Europe. With their tote bags, the immigrants brought along all their old prejudices, and immediately picked up some new ones. An Irishman who came here hating only the Englishmen and Irish Protestants soon hated Poles, Italians, and blacks. A Pole who was free arrived hating only Jews and Russians, but soon learned to hate the Irish, the Italians, and the blacks.

That was another good reason to stay close to home and in your own neighborhood-town and ethnic state. Go that way, past the viaduct, and the wops will jump you, or chase you into Jew town. Go the other way, beyond the park, and the Polacks would stomp on you. Cross those streetcar tracks, and the Micks will shower you with Irish confetti from the brickyards. And who can tell what the niggers might do?

But in the neighborhood, you were safe. At least if you did not cross beyond, say, to the other side of the school. While it might be part of your ethnic state, it was still the edge of another neighborhood, and their gang was just as mean as your gang.

So, for a variety of reasons, ranging from convenience to fear to economics, people stayed in their own neighborhood, loving it, enjoying the closeness, the friendliness, the familiarity, and trying to save enough money to move out.

Into such a self-contained neighborhood was born Richard J. Daley. For his time, and his destiny, he could not have chosen a better place.

His was the great and powerful Irish South Side, bordered on the east by blacks and on the west by a variety of slavs.

The Irish settled in Chicago around 1840 to dig a canal, live in shanties, and work in the industries that followed their strong backs. The area became known as Back of the Yards, because of its greatest wonder—the stockyards. Then the nation's busiest slaughterhouse, it gave meat to the nation, jobs to the South Side, and a stink to the air that was unforgettable.

Daley's neighborhood was Bridgeport, located at the north end of the ethnic state. The people lived in small homes and flats, there were ten Catholic churches, about the same number of smaller Protestant churches, countless saloons, and a natural body of water, known as Bubbly Creek, into which the stockyards dumped wastes and local thugs dumped victims.

In Bridgeport's early days, the people grew cabbage on vacant land in their yards, and it was known for a time as the Cabbage Patch. But by the time Daley was born, most people had stopped raising cabbage and had taken

to raising politicians. Daley was to become the third con-
secutive mayor produced by Bridgeport. It would also
produce an extraordinary number of lesser officeholders,
appointed officials, and, legend says, even more votes than
it had voters.

It was a community that drank out of the beer pail and
ate out of the lunch bucket. The men worked hard in the
stockyards, nearby factories, breweries, and construction
sites. It was a union neighborhood. They bought small
frame homes or rented flats. It had as many Catholic
schools as public schools, and the enrollment at the paroch-
ial schools was bigger.

Daley was born on May 15, 1902, in a flat at 3602
South Lowe, less than a block from where he later lived
as mayor.

His father, Michael, was a short, wiry, quiet man, a
sheet-metal worker. His parents had come from County
Waterford. His mother, Lillian Dunne Daley, had been
born in Bridgeport of parents from Limerick.

When Daley was born, his father was twenty-two and
his mother was thirty. He was their only child.

Daley has said little about his childhood, other than
that it was happy and typical. His mother baked bread
and his father worked hard. His earliest memory was of
being taken into the Church of the Nativity, where his
mother was an energetic volunteer church worker. His
political memories begin with his mother's taking him
along when she joined in women's suffrage marches.

His old friends, such as Judge William Lynch, say he
was always shy, even as a little boy, and that he always
dressed well, better than most of the children in the
neighborhood. "I think the reason he's always had trouble
talking," an old Bridgeport resident said, "was that there
weren't any other children in his home, and his parents
were quiet people. His father never said much and his
mother pretty well ran things. His mother kept an eye on
him. He always had nice clothes, she saw to that. With
only one child, they could afford it."

Daley was enrolled in the elementary school at the
Nativity Church, under the strict discipline of the nuns.
The Nativity Church was the center of the community,
towering over the small homes. The church and the local

political office provided most of the social welfare benefits of the day. Families that were down on their luck could get a small loan, food, a job referral.

Throughout boyhood, Daley always had a part-time or a weekend job. He sold papers at the streetcar stops on Halsted Street and sometimes boarded the cars to sell papers in the aisles. He picked up pocket money by working on a horse-drawn vegetable wagon, running up the back steps with orders.

Bridgeport families, with their low incomes, could not make plans for college educations for their children. If it happened, fine; but it was more realistic to prepare them for a job.

So when Daley finished elementary school, his parents enrolled him at De La Salle Institute, a three-year commercial high school, operated by the Christian Brothers.

The school taught typing, shorthand, bookkeeping and other office skills. Those were the days when men worked as secretaries. While some general academic courses were provided, the diploma was accepted only by Catholic colleges.

The school gave Daley his first glimpse of institutional segregation. Drab and already old looking, it was located in the Negro area east of Bridgeport. The 350 students were white, about ninety percent of them Irish.

The Christian Brothers provided him with another ample dose of discipline and order. "They were good teachers," one of Daley's classmates remembers, "but if you got out of line, they wouldn't hesitate to punch you in the head." One of the teaching brothers, after slamming a student's head into the blackboard, let the brow-sized dent remain in the board for years as a stimulant to learning.

Most of the students did not have to be punched. They came from hard-working families, to whom the fifty dollars a year tuition, ten dollars typewriter rental, and the daily streetcar fare were a substantial investment. To a laborer, it represented three or four pay envelopes. Students brought home weekly report slips to be signed by their parents printed on different colored slips, pink meaning failure, as a hedge against an illiterate parent's being deceived.

The school had little to offer besides a ticket to a job. The sports program was intramural softball in a little courtyard. The lunchroom sold a plate of beans for a nickel. Anybody caught smoking was fined one dollar. Daley never took it up. The students didn't hang around after school because the neighborhood was black, and there were racial fights. Daley arrived and left each day with a group from Bridgeport. Most of the student cliques were along neighborhood lines.

Between the discipline and the course of studies, it was not an easy place for anyone to become a big man on campus. If anybody filled that role, it wasn't Daley.

They remember him as having been "a hard worker . . . maybe a little above average . . . just an average kid . . . short, stocky, even then . . . built like a brick outhouse . . . affable . . . always a heavyweight, not belligerent, but he could handle himself and he had a deep voice."

Only one of his classmates, who later spent many years holding down a desk in City Hall, saw him in a completely different light: "He was a brilliant person, even then. I could see the greatness in him. Everybody could. He got along with everybody. People sought him out. He was a brilliant student. He did everything well. He was an outstanding softball player."

Daley's class graduated in June 1919, and the school accomplished its objective: almost all of the graduates got office work. The school found jobs for some. It had a working relationship with private firms and City Hall, and one youth found himself clerking in a downtown court that specialized in prostitution cases. Few went to college, but some did well in business. And at their reunions many years later, they were unanimous in their satisfaction with their strict, functional education, in their contempt for modern youth and dissent, and in their distrust of blacks.

If June 1919 was a memorable month for Daley's class, the next month was even more memorable for them, and the rest of the South Side.

On July 27, a black youth, swimming off the Twenty-seventh Street beach, made the mistake of drifting south until he was off the Twenty-ninth Street beach. In doing so, he had crossed an invisible line that separated the white and black beaches.

When he tried to come ashore, the whites stoned him, and he swam back out. Black bathers ran to his aide, fights broke out, more stones were thrown, and the black youth drowned.

It wasn't the first such incident on the South Side. Besides the threat they posed in housing and job competition, the blacks had antagonized the heavily Democratic white neighborhoods by voting Republican. They were given credit for Republican Mayor William Thompson's slim victory that spring.

But nothing had ever happened on the scale of the rioting that broke out that oppressively hot day after word of the youth's death swept the black area, and rumors of a black uprising mobilized the whites.

The biggest race war in Chicago's history erupted. It raged for four days and left 15 whites and 23 blacks dead, 178 whites and 342 blacks injured. About one thousand homes were burned.

Daley has never discussed his memories of the riot, but he surely has some, because his neighborhood was part of the battleground. The heaviest rioting took place on the South Side, and most of the deaths and serious injuries were in the Back of the Yards and the adjoining black area.

The Illinois Commission of Human Relations, which conducted a three year study of the riot, said, "Forty-one percent of the clashes occurred in the white neighborhood near the Stockyards, between the South branch of the Chicago River and 55th St."

Dozens of white mobs prowled the streets. Blacks going home were dragged from streetcars, beaten, and killed. Raiding parties drove into black areas and lobbed bombs into homes. The blacks retaliated by killing white delivery men and greeting white raiders with gunfire.

Fighting broke out in the Loop and spilled into the West Side Italian area, which a Negro workman entered on a bike, but left in a box.

The question has been raised by newspapers from time to time: Was young Daley a participant in the violence?

Blacks passing through his neighborhood were beaten within screaming distance of his home. Daley has never answered, or even acknowledged, the question. The 1919 riot itself is something he has never talked about. But if he wasn't part of it, if he sat out his neighborhood's bloody battle, it is certain that some of his friends participated, because Daley belonged to a close-knit neighborhood club known as the Hamburg Social and Athletic Club. And this is what the riot study had to say of the club:

"Responsibility for many attacks was definitely placed by many witnesses upon the 'athletic clubs' including Ragen's Colts, the Hamburgers, Aylwards, Our Flag, Standard . . . and several others. The mobs were made up for the most part of boys between 15 and 22.

"Gangs, particularly of white youths, formed definite nuclei for crowd and mob formations. Athletic clubs supplied the leaders of many gangs."

In later years, Daley described the Hamburgs as something of a cross between the Boy Scouts of America and the YMCA, saying:

"Its purpose was social and athletic and some of the finest athletes, priests, and citizens of Chicago have been members."

And Judge Lynch said: "It was a great debating place. We talked about the issues of the day, national affairs, local politics, and, of course, sports."

But others, looking in from the outside, or from the sidewalk up, saw it in a different way.

A policeman, talking to the riot commission interviewers, said of the Back of the Yards "athletic clubs":

"There is the Canaryville bunch in there and the Hamburg bunch. It is a pretty tough hole."

John Waner, a Republican city politician who was defeated by Daley for mayor in 1967, grew up in the slavic area west of Bridgeport, and he recalls that in the 1920's, "Gee, you'd never think of just walking into their neighborhood, or you'd get the hell knocked out of you by the Hamburgs."

Social and athletic club, made up of men who would be priests and leaders, or a tough, street fighting mob of brawlers?

It was probably both, just as Daley's neighborhood, almost fifty years later, was composed of hard-working churchgoing citizens, who nevertheless poured into his street and became a mob when a black college student moved into a flat.

When the 1919 riots occurred, the Hamburgs had already won neighborhood fame for their street battles with the rival Ragen's Colts from the Canaryville neighborhood to the north. They never had the Colts' reputation for criminality, but were handy with a brick.

The Hamburgs, by then, were a political force in Bridgeport, and the rest of what was then the Thirteenth Ward.

In 1914 the president of the Hamburg Club, Tommy Doyle, twenty-eight, decided to challenge an alderman who had been in office for twenty years.

Doyle won. And according to news accounts of the day, he won because 350 young men from the club went out in teams of ten every night and "campaigned" for him.

Four years later, the Hamburgs helped send Doyle to the state legislature, and another Hamburg hero, big Joe McDonough, was elected to the City Council.

Doyle went on to become a congressman, one of the few to carry a gun in a belt holster, and McDonough in a few years was the leader of the ward and one of the most powerful Democrats in the city.

By 1924, Daley was elected the club's president, and he remained in office for about fifteen years. As mayor, he would appoint old-timer Hamburg members and their sons to some of the city's top administrative posts. The Hamburgs, still with headquarters in a store on Halsted Street, have more power than some of the city's most prestigious private businessmen's clubs. If it never made *Who's Who in America,* it is part of what's what in Chicago.

After graduation, Daley had his last experience with private enterprise. And therein lies a Daley legend.

He is portrayed by his publicists as having been a young "cowboy" in the stockyards, herding cattle on horseback, a Bridgeport John Wayne. For years, the legend goes, he herded cattle during the day, then dragged himself to law school at night, weary but unfaltering in his determination to improve himself. Even Abe Lincoln couldn't have worked harder.

"That is just so much bull," says Benjamin Adamowski, once a friend, and later Daley's most bitter political enemy. "He got on a public payroll almost as soon as he was able to vote, and he's been there since."

It does appear that Adamowski's version of Daley's cowboy years is closer to the truth than the legends.

Daley did go to work in the stockyards after graduation, but his secretarial skills soon had him working at a desk. If he rode horses, it was not a long trail drive.

At twenty-one, he was a precinct captain in McDonough's ward organization and a member of the Hamburgs. Then, as now, being a precinct captain in a solid ward organization usually meant some kind of public payroll job. Add to that the Hamburg status, and you do not have somebody who needed to stomp around in cow dung.

Daley's memory gets foggy when asked about this period. The closest he has ever come to being specific about his period of stockyard employment is "about three or four years."

That would bring him to about twenty or twenty-one years of age, which is when he found a place on McDonough's lap and became his personal ward secretary and a protégé. It was also the time when William Dever, a Democrat, was elected a reform mayor. Since Chicago reforms begin with the firing of city workers from the other parties, the Democrats were grabbing all the patronage jobs. This, then, is when Daley apparently got his first City Hall job, as a clerk in the City Council. He would be on public payrolls for the next forty-eight years, at least.

If the regular pay was important to him, the opportunity to learn was of even greater long-range significance.

As McDonough's personal secretary in the ward organization, he could observe political science, as applied at the local level: the doling out of patronage jobs to the deserving and the firing of the undeserving; the helping of friends through the fix and the punishing of enemies through pressure from city inspectors; the adjustment of a case at the police station; the adding up of votes so they come out the right way; and all the other skills a ward leader must have and not get caught at.

Then down to the clerical job in City Hall for more learning. The first lesson is always the same: never repeat what you see or hear, or somebody might get indicted.

The City Council, where Daley was put to work shuffling papers and fetching coffee, was where many of the party powerhouses were. He was able to observe how driveway permits were sold to property owners, how and why rate increases were granted to utilities and public transportation lines, how rezoning could send a piece of property spiraling in value with the stroke of a pen, and where the bottles were kept in the cloak room.

It had to be a jaw-dropping experience for a shy, churchgoing youth from a proper family, all those cigar-chomping bandits sitting among their spittoons and dividing up the town.

The city had just come off eight years of rule by raucous Big Bill Thompson, who had put up buildings and bridges, widened streets, and made countless contractors happy. They, in turn, made countless politicians happy.

He also made the gangsters happy by giving them the run of the town, and they made the Police Department happy by giving them a piece of the profit. Everybody was happy except the people being shot and the citizens who thought things were getting a bit outlandish, even for Chicago.

Reform was demanded by the civic leaders in 1923, and Thompson didn't run for a third term. And that brought in Mayor Dever, a judge, and by Chicago standards, a decent man. He set out to reform City Hall, but there was only so much he could do, since most of the members of his party considered reform to be the redirecting of graft from Republicans to themselves.

Dever did manage to get Al Capone out of Chicago, after Thompson had almost given him the key to the city. Capone moved his headquarters to Cicero, a nearby suburb. He promptly went into Cicero politics, running his own slate of candidates. On election day, three people were killed, several were kidnapped, many were beaten, and Capone's candidates won. The Syndicate took over Cicero and never completely let go. It still has its strip of bars where gambling and whoring are unnoticed. The only thing they won't tolerate in Cicero are Negroes.

From Cicero, Capone had no difficulty running his bootleg empire, which brought in millions of dollars a week, and the killings went on, although Dever managed to close down hundreds of speakeasies.

As much as Chicagoans wanted reform, they wanted their bootleg gin more, so after four years of Dever, they returned Thompson to power. Capone came back downtown and had things his own way until the federal government imprisoned him for tax evasion. He came out wasting away with syphilis, but Capone, with Thompson's tacit consent, had built the model American municipal crime syndicate. His successors never again ran the town, as he did, but they always had a piece of the action.

These were Chicago's "Roaring Twenties." And through those fast-paced years plodded young Richard Daley.

During the day he worked in City Hall. After work, he went to DePaul University's School of Law, four nights a week, 6 P.M. to 8 P.M. The rest of his time was taken up with ward politics and the Hamburg Club athletics. He managed the club's softball team.

Another boyhood friend, Steven Bailey, who became head of the Plumbers' Union, said, "I used to go out dancing at night, but Dick would go home and hit the books."

One of Daley's fellow students was Louis Wexler, a Russian-born immigrant, who got off the boat and zipped through elementary and high school in four years.

"Daley was a nice fellow, very quiet, a hard worker, and always neatly dressed. He never missed a class and always got there on time. But there was nothing about him that would make him stand out, as far as becoming something special in life. Even then, he misused the language so that you noticed it. He had trouble expressing himself and his grammar wasn't good." But thirty years later, Daley's grammar was good enough to say "yes" when Wexler appealed to their old night school ties, and Wexler became a judge.

If the pace was plodding, the future, at least, held promise. In Alderman McDonough, the ward leader, Daley had a political godfather with upward mobility and long coattails.

McDonough had wisely allied himself in the City

Council with Anton (Tony) Cermak, a one-time coal miner who had become the political leader of the Bohemian community. Uneducated, tough, crude, but politically brilliant, Cermak had the gall to challenge the traditional South Side Irish domination of the Democratic party. More than gall, he had the sense to count up all the Irish votes, then he counted all the Italians, Jews, Germans, Poles, and Bohemians. The minority Irish domination didn't make sense to him. He organized a city-wide saloon keepers' league, dedicated to fighting closing laws and prohibition. With the saloon keepers behind him, he couldn't be stopped. He became president of the Cook County Board, took over the party machinery, and ran for mayor in 1931.

Most of the South Side Irish leaders thought of Cermak as the worst thing since the potato famine. They didn't realize that he was doing them a favor while cuffing them about. He didn't realize it either.

By creating the ethnically balanced ticket, something new, he put together the most powerful political machine in Chicago history. It is the direct ancestor of the organization Daley inherited.

Soon after Cermak was elected mayor, he was on a speaking platform in Miami when a mad assassin took a shot at President Roosevelt and got him instead.

The Chicago Machine gave him a hero's funeral, the biggest in city history, changed the name of Twenty-second Street to Cermak Road, wiped away its tears, and then the South Side put Ed Kelly in as mayor and let Pat Nash run the party. The famine was over.

Two years earlier, however, Cermak had slated his friend McDonough as the candidate for county treasurer. If McDonough won, Daley knew it would be his ticket out of the City Council, to a job in the treasurer's office.

He worked hard, as did the rest of Bridgeport, to bring in the vote for McDonough, throwing back his head and leading rallies in McDonough's personal campaign song:

Whataya gonna do for McDonough?
Whataya gonna do for YOU?
Are ya gonna carry your precinct?

Are you gonna be true blue?
Whenever ya wanted a favor,
McDonough was ready to do.
Whataya gonna do for McDonough,
after what he done for you?

McDonough and the rest of the Democratic ticket won easily, and Daley got his desk in the treasurer's office as an administrative assistant. It paid better and it was another chance to learn. The council had taught him what it had to offer, and now he could immerse himself in the complexities of tax collection, banking of county funds, and the management of a large patronage office.

Somebody had to do the work, because McDonough didn't want to. To McDonough, a stubby 280-pounder, the charm of elective office was not mucking about with papers and figures. The office meant more jobs, more power. The management was left to trusted and skilled assistants. McDonough had other interests that took his time. He loved the horses, and never missed a Kentucky Derby.

When his long absences from the County Building became noticeable to the press, McDonough offered a novel excuse: because he was known to be a generous and soft-hearted man, people were constantly coming to him for loans, jobs, and other favors; therefore, he said, the only way he could get any work done was to stay away from his office.

Daley eagerly took over much of the responsibility of the county treasurer, although the voters didn't know it. And he may have acquired an added incentive for wanting to make a good showing. The summer before the election, he had met a young lady.

By all accounts, Daley was not a lady's man. Shy and reserved around men, he was a paralytic near women. The glib tongue of the Irish had been swallowed somewhere in his ancestry.

His idea of a big time was a Hamburg softball game and a few beers and some poker at The Pump on Halsted Street or Babe Connelly's Bar on Thirty-seventh Street.

It was at a softball game that a casual acquaintance named Lloyd Guilfoyle introduced Daley, then twenty-eight, to his sister, Eleanor Guilfoyle, nineteen, a paint company secretary.

The Guilfoyles were a large family from neighboring Canaryville, and Miss Guilfoyle had an upbringing and education as Catholic as Daley's.

Shyness aside, Daley was a handsome man in his youth, with strong clean features, thick black hair, and an erect posture. He was stocky, but not fat.

The couple began keeping company in 1930, and six years after they met, they were married. Daley's pace was consistent in all matters.

In 1934, Daley got his long sought law degree, but he didn't go into private practice. During the Depression, LaSalle Street was full of good lawyers who didn't have the price of lunch, but Daley had a regular paycheck. The legal knowledge was useful, and the degree and license another step forward, but practicing law was not his ambition. He has never practiced it, although he and Lynch had a firm between 1946 and 1955. Of Daley as a lawyer, Tom Keane, his council leader and a rich lawyer himself, says:

"Daley wouldn't know what the inside of a courtroom looks like. He never practiced law. Lynch handled all the firm's work. All Daley ever cared about was politics, and he spent his time running for office."

In his pursuit of elective office it looked like a long wait in 1934. Despite the Democrats' control of state, county, and city offices, there wasn't much open at Daley's level. Tom Doyle, the hard-drinking congressman, had returned from Washington to replace McDonough as alderman. And Doyle was only forty-eight. McDonough was a mere forty-five. Ahead of Daley in ward organization influence was Babe Connelly, a saloon keeper, bookie, and former speakeasy operator who was only forty-three. It could be years before something opened up. How long can a man be happy as president of the Hamburg Club?

It all changed quickly. In 1934, McDonough was stricken with pneumonia and died. His funeral was the biggest since Cermak's. Thousands filled the streets outside the Church of the Nativity and watched every big shot, from the governor down, mourn him. One thousand cars went to the cemetery. The biggest names in politics were his honorary pallbearers. But Daley and Babe Connelly carried the casket.

A year later, Alderman Doyle got pneumonia and he died as quickly as had McDonough. Connelly replaced Doyle in the City Council. The turnover in ward leadership was complete. Babe Connelly was now the boss, and Daley and a few other ambitious young men were right behind him.

Meanwhile, Daley was working for three more county treasurers, and an interesting trio they were.

When McDonough died, the party asked Thomas Nash, a first cousin of Party Chairman Pat Nash, to complete the unexpired term. Tom Nash was a ward leader and a prosperous criminal lawyer who defended Capone and other gangsters. And if the clients died of an overdose of bullets, he was not too proud to go to their funerals. It wasn't uncommon for Chicago politicians to join in the mourning at the funerals of gangsters with aldermen weeping and judges praying. There was good reason for them to weep and pray, as they had to deal with somebody new. Tom Nash's law firm produced more Chicago and state judges than any other.

Then there was Robert M. Sweitzer, a veteran officeholder, who became county treasurer in December 1934. Within a year he was found to have lost $453,000 in county funds in an unsuccessful private business venture—he had tried to manufacture synthetic coal briquettes. He was ousted, tried, pleaded good intentions, and was acquitted.

This brought in Joe Gill, another ward boss, who is believed to have gone on his first public payroll before the turn of the century; he lived long enough to spend his twilight years as a park commissioner and, in 1968, to tell the strange Yippie creatures that they could not camp in the parks during the Democratic Convention.

In 1936, Daley's big break finally came. Again somebody died. This time it was an elderly state legislator, David Shanahan, who had been speaker of the Illinois House. He died only fifteen days before the November 3 elections, with his name already on the ballots. It seemed like a terrible waste to elect a dead man to office, especially in the legislative district that included Bridgeport, where there were so many live ones.

It was too late to reprint the ballots, so the Machine organized a write-in campaign for Daley. The precinct captains did their jobs, getting eighty-six hundred people to write in his name, and on November 4, 1936, Daley had won his first elective office.

The only thing that kept the victory from being perfect was the fact that Shanahan had been a Republican, running unopposed. So Daley's name had to be written in on the Republican side of the ballot. Richard Daley was elected to his first public office as, of all things, a Republican.

In fact, when he got to the legislature, he had to spend his first morning on the Republican side of the aisle. Ironically, the Democratic minority leader was Adamowski, his future enemy, and Adamowski offered the resolution to let Daley come sit among the Democrats.

The Republicans, still angered by the Bridgeport opportunism that cheated them of a seat, made Daley suffer for it. Their leader pointed a long finger at Daley and said: "I don't care about the resolution. I want to know where Representative Daley wants to sit. Where do you want to sit, Representative Daley?"

Daley pointed at the Democrats and, in a soft voice, said, "There."

"Then go on over there," the Republican leader barked, "because we don't want you over here."

He did, gratefully. And two years later somebody else in his neighborhood dropped dead and Daley took his place in the state Senate, going in by the front door, finally, as a Democrat.

Chapter III

KUNSTLER: Mayor Daley, I show you D-242 for identification and ask you if you can identify the top letter.

WITNESS: What kind of identification?

KUNSTLER: Who is the letter from?

WITNESS: A district judge of the Northern District of Illinois.

KUNSTLER: It is a federal judge, is that correct?

WITNESS: Right.

KUNSTLER: And it is addressed to you, is it not?

WITNESS: Yes, I have many comments from people all over the country with comments of people who have commented on our . . .

KUNSTLER: Your honor, can I ask the witness to answer it?

HOFFMAN: All right. Anything after "yes" may go out and the jury is directed to disregard any word after the word "yes."

KUNSTLER: Now, the letter is signed "Abe." Do you know who "Abe" is?

FORAN: I object to that. That is a leading and suggestive question.

Abe.

For Abraham.

As in Abraham Lincoln.

As in Abraham Lincoln Marovitz.

And he never lets you forget it. The walls of his chambers in the U.S. courthouse are covered with a hundred faces of Lincoln. Where the paintings leave off, the books about Lincoln begin. On the tables are busts of Lincoln Quotations of Lincoln are squeezed into the spaces between the pictures. It could be a Lincoln museum. In his courtroom, a picture of Lincoln hangs on the wall.

It used to be plain Abe. As a kid on the crowded West Side, where his parents ran a corner candy store and the big family lived in the back, it was even Little Abe. Then as now, he was tiny, but athletically lean, a featherweight club fighter who hoped to grow into a Jewish champ like his hero Benny Leonard. He grew up, instead, to be a federal judge and so close a friend to the mayor that he administered the oath of office each time Richard J. Daley began a new term.

It was still Abe, or A.L., or Abraham L., when he was a young criminal lawyer and a state senator. But now, a Daley-arranged appointee to the federal bench, it is Abraham Lincoln Marovitz.

"Don't believe everything you hear about me and the, uh, Mafia," says Federal Judge Abraham Lincoln Marovitz. "You see, in my younger days I wanted to make a lot of money. I was very ambitious to become a big success. So I defended people who were some of the dirtiest, the most disgusting people around. They were the kind of people I would never have had anything to do with if they weren't my clients, but I was young and eager for success, so I defended them."

There was Gus Winkler, a Capone gunman, often credited with being on the safe end of the machine gun at the famous St. Valentine's Day Massacre in 1929. It was embarrassing when a police phone-tapper heard criminal lawyer Abe Marovitz answer the daily check-in call from client Winkler with a light-hearted "Well, what bank did you rob today?"

There was Willie Bioff, big-time pimp and Syndicate extortionist, who found that the way to make a million was to find somebody who had a million and threaten to kill him. It caused talk when State Senator Abe Marovitz tore himself away from the legislature to counsel client Bioff. That was a long time ago, and the talk would have faded but for Judge Abraham Lincoln Marovitz's peculiar habit of being seen with men who earn their living accepting big bets, which is not legal in most places outside of Las Vegas.

And there was the matter of his personal bailiff of many years, a West Side politician who has a brother called "Cockeyed" and another brother known as "One Ear," both of whom were outstanding Mafia figures despite their physical shortcomings. "Over the years you get to know so many people, and some old friends go all the way back to boyhood," is the way the judge explains some of his strange acquaintances. When the subject comes up, he can almost read the nagging thought, and answers, "In all my years on the state and federal bench, I have never accepted a nickel, a penny, to influence a decision of mine or any other judge." Then he shrugs and raises his brow. "But friendship . . . ?"

It's been said that nobody in Chicago has as many friends as Judge Abraham Lincoln Marovitz. A bachelor, he has long chummed with show business people and enjoyed nightclub society. He has friends in sports, politics, business, the church, law, and they are all over the country. The walls of a smaller room in his chambers are covered with row upon row of pictures of his more famous friends, all bearing a warm inscription.

Helping and remembering friends is important to him, because he was helped. He was still a young club fighter when an influential politician-lawyer on the West Side took a liking to him and put him through law school. The same sponsor then got him a job as the youngest assistant prosecutor in Cook County history.

Later, another sponsor ran him for the legislature and boosted him toward the state courts. And finally Daley put him on the federal bench. He values friendship and recognizes its responsibilities. Because he has so many friends, the phones in his chambers are constantly ringing. When he is hearing a case, the phone messages stack up. Some friend is always calling him from somewhere, and he will break away from office visitors to chat with them, as he did with the man who called from California.

"Hi, Bob. Fine, fine, how are you? Good. How's the weather out there? Good. What can I do for you, Bob? Uh huh . . . uh huh . . . I see. Bob, you know I won't give you a line of bunk on this. I can't do anything for you. Let me tell you how I feel about it. I don't like what these kids are doing today on the campuses. I worked hard for my education. I worked hard for everything I have. Now these kids want to burn down the campuses. I don't understand that attitude and I don't approve of what they're doing. What? Uh huh. I see. Bob, I won't give you a line of bunk, I won't do anything on this. Now, he's a very able man, Bob, and I'm sure she'll be treated fairly. Uh huh, fine. Everything else OK? Good talking to you, Bob. 'By."

Being a man who worked hard for what he has, it is natural that he would write a letter to his old friend, Dick, signing it Abe, and telling him he supported the way the mayor handled the disturbances in 1968. They are very old friends. With the Hatch Act forbidding federal judges to do any politicking, what other judge spends every election night in the charmed inner office of Democratic Headquarters, sitting with Daley as the returns come in? That's friendship.

"You know when I first met Dick? It was way back when I was a young assistant state's attorney and he was clerking in the City Council. That's how far back I know him. But where I really got to know him was in the legislature. He served one term in the House, then he was elected to the Senate, and that's where I was. We were a real minority. There were twelve of us and thirty-nine Republicans. I saw a lot of potential in him right away. He worked hard. I thought right from the beginning that he had an amazing knowledge of finance and municipal budgeting and taxation. He was on the appropriations committee, and things that confused me, he'd explain so that they were understandable.

"Dick went to church every morning in Springfield. He's a daily communicant, you know, but not the kind who wears it on his sleeve. A lot of guys in Springfield were sleeping with secretaries, but not Dick. And the buck meant little to him. He stayed away from that, and the nightlife. We'd take long walks together, all over Springfield. That was his recreation.

"Not many people remember this, and I'm sure I have it somewhere in my files, but when I was leaving the

Senate to go into the marines in 1943, I made my final speech and I said, 'I will return to help elect my friend Dick Daley mayor of the city of Chicago.' I think I was the first person to ever suggest publicly that he would be mayor someday. I said it on the Senate floor.

"When I came back after the war, I helped get him slated for sheriff. Ed Kelly had asked him to run, and Dick wanted it, too. I remember the day he was slated, the three of us, Dick, myself, and Bill Lynch went to his home and told his family about it. Dick's mother didn't like the idea. She said, 'I didn't raise my son to be a policeman.' She was a wonderful woman, his mother. A typical, strong, Irishwoman and there was no question who ruled the roost. His father was a quiet man, but he was surprisingly well informed on current issues. I remember when we were sitting around talking about Israel one evening, he made several remarks that showed he knew what the situation was. He even bought a thousand-dollar bond from me.

"It was a terrible blow to Dick when he lost for sheriff. I think the thing that beat him was the papers saying that electing him would be the same as electing Ed Kelly, and did the voters want that? After he lost, he felt just miserable, so Lynch and I took him down to New Orleans to cheer him up. He hates losing."

With Marovitz and Daley, Benjamin Adamowski took part in those long evening walks through Springfield. The same era, the same people, the same places as seen through the eyes and memory of Adamowski, already a rising young Democrat when Daley arrived in Springfield:

"I remember those walks. Abe Marovitz was always saying, 'Some day the three of us will run Chicago, a Pole, an Irishman, and a Jew.' Abe was always saying that. But Daley never said anything. I never once heard him say a word about where he wanted to go. Actually, he didn't say much of anything. He rarely said anything on the Senate floor. He was very quiet, humble, and respectful of everyone, and he developed a reputation for being good on revenue matters, but that was about all.

"Most of the time he kept to himself, stayed in his hotel room, and worked hard. In Springfield you could tell real fast which men were there for girls, games, and graft. He wasn't. I'll tell you how he made it. He made it through sheer luck and by attaching himself to one guy after another and then stepping over them. His ward committeeman in those days was Babe Connelly. Babe was always pushing Daley out front. He sent him to Springfield, pushed him for the better jobs. Then, when Daley got a chance, he squeezed Connelly out.

"When I got back from the service and found out he was going to run for sheriff, I couldn't believe it. I told him: 'What in the hell do you want to do that for? You can't help but get dirty in that office. Everybody does.' He told me Kelly wanted him to run, and that Lynch thought it was a good idea. But he wanted it. He would have run for anything, he was that eager for it, that hungry for the power."

Marovitz and Adamowski agree on one thing: Daley shied away from the many pleasures of Springfield during his eleven years as a state legislator. The women, a harem of state employees, were known as "the monkey girls, because they hang on to their jobs with their tails." Some legislators set up housekeeping when the biennial gatherings began and played house for the six-month sessions. Many of the girls would come to the railroad stations to kiss their paunchy senators goodbye on Friday and hello on the following Tuesday. One West Side Republican, a bombastic moralist, is still remembered for hauling his love-nest furniture across town on his back after a spat with his mistress.

Money was there for those who wanted it, and many did. Lobbyists expected to pay for votes. Their generosity was matched by the legislators' greed. If a day passed without profit, some legislators would dream up a "fetcher" bill. A "fetcher" bill would, say, require that all railroad tracks in the state be relaid six inches farther apart. It would "fetch" a visit from a lobbyist, bearing a gift.

For the squeamish, there was the lobbyists' card game. The limit varied, but some nights a legislator was guaranteed winnings up to one thousand dollars. After that, he was on his own, but the thousand dollars was a cinch. He did not have to tell his wife he was a grafter, just a lucky poker player.

Every night was like New Year's Eve, the hotel bars echoing with laughter and song, the chomping of steaks, the happy giggles of the young typists, and the sound of the cash registers ringing up the lobbyists' money. There was little effort at pretense. Everybody knew the next man's appetites and his price. Daley knew, of course, down to the men in his Chicago delegation. But so long as he wasn't part of it, his conscience felt clean. He worked hard, took his long walks, listened to the gossip without offering anything in return, and made his nightly calls to Sis, home on Lowe Avenue. They had built their pink house in 1939, and the children were being born. Everybody agreed that Senator Daley was a virtuous man.

Senator Botchy Conners, part of the Kelly-Nash delegation and a carnivore from the honky-tonk North Side, said, "You can't give that guy a nickel, that's how honest he is."

Daley's moral code was emerging: Thou shalt not steal, but thou shalt not blow the whistle on anybody who does.

By 1942 Daley was Mayor Kelly's man in Springfield, handling city-interest legislation, while back in Chicago, Kelly and Party Chairman Nash were running a town almost as open as in Bill Thompson's days. Bookie wire rooms were visible from the streets. Political hacks were mismanaging city agencies. Although some Democrats objected to the Kelly-Nash leadership, and there were occasionally primary fights and maverick movements, Daley rejected them and worked for the organization, regardless of its excesses, and it, in turn, rewarded him. Shortly after he went to Springfield, he had been given one of the most politically sensitive nonelective jobs in county government: that of Cook County comptroller. This put him on two public payrolls, the county and the state, and assured him of an adequate income.

More important, it was a position of party trust, and a rare source of information and knowledge. As comptroller, he alone kept the books for all of Cook County government. He knew exactly who was on every payroll and at what salary. This could be fascinating information, since a flunky who carries a politician's coat might very well be on the payroll of the Highway Department as an engineer. More important, every penny of the millions of dollars

spent by the many county agencies was recorded in his
books. He knew which contractors were favored, which
public works projects were being loaded down with
"extras" that sent the final cost soaring far beyond the
low bid price, which supply companies were favored at
the County Hospital, and all the other secrets that were
open to a man who knew how to read the figures. They
gave him the job because he could be trusted.

Because of his reputation for personal honesty, his
decision to run for sheriff in 1946 surprised some of his
acquaintances. The Cook County Sheriff's Department
was a notorious money pot. The sheriff's police were supposed to patrol the roads and residential areas in the
sizable unincorporated parts of the suburbs and were
empowered to enter any town if local police weren't doing
their job. They spent most of their time, however, shaking
down motorists and making collections at suburban bars
and brothels. Since a sheriff couldn't succeed himself,
most of them got in, got it, and got out. Few left without
being the subject of scandal. It was a natural and easy
target for newspapers.

Nevertheless, it was an elective office on the county-
wide ticket. And Daley, at forty-four, had yet to run for
anything beyond his local legislative district. Despite the
risks, the office provided a large patronage force of policemen, process servers, the staff at the medieval county jail,
elevator operators, janitors and scrubwomen, and a
number of court employees. The Central Committee would
retain most of them, but as the officeholder he would get
to fill at least a few.

Kelly wanted him on the ticket because he was trying
to shore up his sagging reputation with the voters. Pat
Nash had died in 1943, and now Kelly was running both
the party and city government, and doing badly at both
jobs. Daley received little attention from the press while
in Springfield, but what he got was good, and most important, he had never been in trouble. Candidates who
could make that statement were scarce.

By agreeing to run, Daley gave up his Senate seat and
angered some of the old guard on the South Side. They
didn't want him to go on the ticket because they were, at
the time, feuding with Kelly. But since they were always

feuding with somebody, and Kelly was still party boss, Daley took the chance.

None of the inner machinations mattered, however, because the Democrats took a beating and Daley was defeated by an equally Irish candidate named Elmer Michael Walsh, who had the added advantage of being a newly-returned war veteran. Daley wasn't the only Democrat with problems, though, and while he brooded with Marovitz and Lynch in New Orleans, the party chiefs looked for a way to save themselves. All across the country, city machines were falling apart, and none looked closer to collapse than Chicago's.

It wasn't merely that Kelly had opened the town. Chicagoans enjoy their vices. But he had let it become so obvious that the civic leaders were complaining. Also, basic city services were declining. Garbage collection and street cleaning were haphazard, public transportation was a mess. Worst of all, he had committed the gravest of political sins, next to losing an election: he had allowed politics to creep, to gallop, into the schools. The school board was loaded with party hacks, and what they weren't carrying off, they were wasting. The PTA had demanded that the school superintendent be replaced, and the superintendent airily responded that he "couldn't care less" what the PTA wanted.

Jacob Arvey, just back from the war, was asked to take over as party chairman. Arvey, an attorney and for years an alderman, was leader of the West Side Jewish ghetto and during the thirties had provided the most one-sided returns for Roosevelt of any ward in the country. Several cuts above most ward bosses in intelligence and imagination, he set out to save what Cermak had created.

His first major step was to convince Kelly that he couldn't win and had to step aside. Arvey, Al Horan, a West Side ward boss, and Joe Gill went to his office to tell him. Kelly wouldn't believe it, so right there in City Hall they ran a phone survey for him, calling random names from the phone book and asking them if they would vote for Kelly again. Kelly was unlucky—the random calls didn't turn up any bookies or pimps. He grudgingly agreed to step aside. Next came the problem of finding a candidate. At first, they thought about running one of the other ward leaders but Kelly said, "If you're going to run one of them, you might as well run me again." The Republicans were expected to run a blue-ribbon reformer, so the Democrats decided to do the same. Running a reformer was risky, because he might take things seriously and run amuck, but it would be better to have their own reformer than a Republican reformer, because they could get rid of their own when the time was right.

They selected Martin J. Kennelly, a tall white-haired, respectable businessman. Like Kelly, and Daley, Kennelly was born in Bridgeport. Unlike them, he managed to grow up without learning much about politics, pressing out to make a sizable fortune in the moving and storage business. He had served on numerous civic committees and dabbled on the fringes of politics, mainly at the name-dropping level.

The Republicans were coming on strong. Or at least the voters were out to punish City Hall. In the aldermanic elections preceding the mayoralty by five weeks, seventeen Republicans were elected. The disaster was so widespread that even Bridgeport and the rest of the Eleventh Ward elected a Republican alderman.

When the election for mayor was held, however, the Republicans reverted to form and ran a lackluster candidate. Martin Kennelly won easily, ending fourteen years of steady employment for Ed Kelly. Kelly swore Kennelly in, and he also swore under his breath. Since the Republicans ran a nobody, Kelly was sure he could have won after all.

From the shambles of the aldermanic elections and the final collapse of the Kelly-Nash leadership, Daley walked out even stronger. As always, death or disaster provided him, the organization man, with an opening above.

In the summer of 1947, he began easing Babe Connelly out as committeeman of the Eleventh Ward. Connelly was told that if he didn't step aside, he'd be opposed by Daley the following year, when committeemen stood for election by registered Democrat voters. If Connelly couldn't re-elect himself to the City Council, he didn't deserve ward leadership, Daley reasoned. So Connelly announced that he was retiring for reasons of "health and other conditions." His health was so feeble that he went to Florida and lived for six more years. When he died, they found more than seventy thousand dollars in small bills in his safe-deposit box, a tidy sum for a Depression-era tavern keeper.

Daley, at last, was where he had wanted to be for the many years he had waited and worked. He was finally a member of the Cook County Democratic Central Committee, one of the fifty city ward committeemen and thirty suburban township committeemen who ran the party. He was not just another member, but much more. As the leader of a ward that had been, and would again be, one of the biggest vote producers for the party, he was part of the inner circle within the committee, made up of the leaders of the true "Machine" wards, who could always be counted on to deliver a big majority. In the outer circle were the suburban committeemen and those who struggled in the city's few Republican wards.

He was now in the position to assert himself when openings for public office occurred. He wouldn't have to run for sheriff again, that was for sure. Earlier that year, he had missed a chance for appointment to the prestigious federal post of the United States attorney for northern Illinois, because, as Arvey later explained, "He didn't have enough legal experience." Daley had, in fact, only recently gone into private practice with his friend Lynch. Lynch, as a practicing attorney, provided the experience. Daley, as a politician with a growing reputation, provided the clients with a practical reason to bring him their business. This was the graceful and legitimate way to profit from politics. As Daley later told a young Bridgeport legislator who was going to Springfield for his first session, and who had a small real estate business, "Don't take a nickel; just hand them your business card." Besides the law cases from businessmen and private citizens who felt more secure in the hands of a political law firm, there were other plums. Lynch would be thrown legal work by government offices, and would later become the chief lawyer for the Chicago Transit Authority. Daley was free of financial problems, to pursue power.

Arvey, having saved City Hall with the election of Kennelly, began planning ahead to the 1948 general election.

He decided to use the same formula and, despite protests from the always dissatisfied South Side, he pushed through the slating of two fresh faces for the top offices: Paul Douglas, a University of Chicago economist who had become the City Council's resident intellectual, and Adlai Stevenson, member of a fine Illinois family, wit and orator.

They amazed everyone by winning in a landslide, helping Harry Truman squeak through in Illinois. Arvey was hailed as a genius, although some still contend that he and the others figured that it would be a Republican year, so they might as well let a couple of do-gooder liberals take the lumps. The South Side crowd, as always, found something to be angry about: if a couple of newcomers could win easily, then some of their own could have done almost as well.

The victory opened another rung on the ladder to Daley, who had brought the Eleventh Ward in big. Now as devoted to Chairman Arvey as he had been to Chairman Kelly and Chairman Nash, he stepped forward to share in the spoils. He even helped pass around the spoils. After eight years of a Republican governor, state government was infested with Republicans. The Democrats set up a committee to fire them and bring in Democrats, and Daley took part in the gleeful task. ·

More important, Stevenson needed someone in his cabinet who could serve as a link between the governor's mansion and the legislature. It was impossible for Stevenson, the patrician intellectual, and somebody like Sen. Botchy Conners, a spittoon kicker, to get past their first hello. They needed an interpreter. Daley, with his legislative background and understanding of the ward heeler's needs, was the choice for the job. Daley was appointed to Stevenson's cabinet as state director of revenue.

The appointment brought him, for the first time, widespread press coverage and something of an image as a "new-breed" young Democrat in the Stevenson mold. It wasn't totally accurate, because Daley was carefully maintaining his close ties with the old-timers, and pursuing his personal moral code of pretending not to see their capers, but it made nice reading for the family. Daley applied his accounting skills to his new job as revenue director, instituting procedural reforms that brought further praise in the papers and helped him erase the Kelly-Nash stigma. His name was even turning up in columns of friendly political writers as a possible choice to someday succeed Kennelly. When asked about his ambitions, Daley just blushed and said his ambition was to do his best in the job he had. Then he would resume looking for a bigger job.

It came in 1950. Again, somebody died. This time it was the county clerk, with less than a year left of his four-year term. Stevenson didn't want Daley to leave, but he went, taking over a white-collar office of some three hundred patronage workers. As soon as he was in, he began looking ahead to the November elections—but not for the same office. He wanted something even bigger.

A Republican held the office of County Board president, easily second only to the office of mayor in political power. Daley began seeking support to be slated as the candidate. But the South Side clique had other ideas; they were grooming John Duffy, a ward leader and florist who looked like Popeye the Sailor, to succeed Kennelly, and they wanted him to make the jump from the County Board presidency. This time they prevailed, and Daley agreed to be slated for county clerk.

Once again, disaster struck the party, with nothing but benefits for Daley. The disaster was walking around on the flat feet of one Daniel (Tubbo) Gilbert, their candidate for sheriff. Gilbert, in his early days a union arm-twister, had switched to the more lucrative field of police work and had used political contacts to rise through the ranks to captain. He then moved into the county prosecutor's office, as head of the investigative staff, where he became a shadowy political power, virtually running the office regardless of who the elected state's attorney was.

Only days before the election, a reporter obtained a copy of secret testimony Gilbert had given to a Senate crime committee. The committee discovered that Gilbert, on a humble public servant's salary, had become amazingly wealthy, and they wanted to know how he did it. A man has to say something at a time like that, so Gilbert told them he did it through shrewd business investments and by placing sizable bets on sporting events with big-time Chicago gamblers.

When the story hit the papers, Gilbert was dubbed the "World's Richest Cop," and whatever municipal pride that stirred was buried under a flood of angry votes. On election night, the party leaders alternated between swearing at Gilbert and giving Arvey, who had slated him, dirty looks. Gilbert dragged down much of the ticket with him, including the U.S. Senate majority leader, who was beaten by a syrup-voiced congressman from downstate named Everett Dirksen, and the candidates for the county board presidency, county treasurer, and other lesser offices.

It was a blow to the party, but yet another step forward for Daley. He managed to win his election as county clerk, while competitors for party leadership were knocked off, including the South Side's man Duffy. Like a funeral-goer, Daley joined in the gloom and mourning, but it sure felt good to be alive.

Chairman Arvey, hailed as the genius who saved the machine by slating Kennelly, Douglas, and Stevenson, was now the idiot who slated Tubbo Gilbert. In the silence of the Morrison Hotel headquarters, Arvey waited for somebody, anybody, to tell him it was just one of those bad breaks and not to worry about it. Arvey, knowing he was being blamed, was hoping for a vote of confidence. Nobody offered it, so he finally said, "I think I'm going to resign." Then he went to California to take a vacation and wait for somebody to call and ask him to change his mind—Joe Gill, Al Horan, Daley. Nobody called, so that was it; he was out. And Daley, who had the support of Stevenson, the unwary Kennelly, Gill, Horan, and others, was close to being in as chairman. But it wasn't time yet. If he went after it then, the South Side crowd would put up a fight, and after a bad state and county election and with city elections coming up in 1951, it wasn't time for a party squabble. It was agreed that Gill, a party elder whom nobody could object to, would keep the seat warm for Daley until the time was right.

"Dick could have become chairman in 1951," Edward J. Barrett, a North Side ward leader, later recalled, "but I told him he should wait because all he'd do is work his can off for Kennelly and then Kennelly wouldn't do a damn thing for him anyway."

This was probably good advice. Kennelly had not been

the kind of reform mayor the Democrats wanted. They had hoped that he would launch great public works projects, get a building boom going. This looks good to the voters, impresses the civic leaders, brings whopping business to friendly contractors, and requires zoning changes, building permits, and other lucrative services.

Instead, he became preoccupied with civil service and tried to put more and more city employees under its protection. This is deadly for a political machine that lives through patronage. He had tightened the basic city services, forced the bookies to become a little less obvious, and removed some of the louts from school management. He had stopped the city from going backwards, as it had been moving under Kelly, but it was not going forward either. Kennelly was not a dynamic or imaginative mayor. The part of the job he liked best was standing up at grand civic functions and bathing in the applause. He was also very big for ribbon cutting and waving to people who recognized him in his black limousine.

As Arvey later put it: "He was the most inept man I ever met. I can't understand how he ever became a success in business. He was honest, and if you laid something out in front of him, he might understand, but he had so little talent. They said Stevenson was indecisive. They should have tried working with Kennelly."

A police captain, testifying at a City Council budget hearing while Kennelly was still mayor, put it even more neatly: "The trouble with Mayor Kennelly is that the only thing he learned in the moving business is never to lift the heavy end."

But the organization was stuck. Despite his shortcomings, the voters liked him. He had an honest, grandfatherly manner, and they still remembered the Kelly-Nash days. An effort to dump him would be viewed as a blow by the Machine against reform, and Kennelly might win in a primary fight. The organization had to run him again, and pretend they enjoyed it. And that they did—except for one man, Cong. William Dawson, the leader of the black wards.

Dawson had been nursing a grudge even more intense than that of the others. Shortly after Kennelly took office in 1947, unfamiliar policemen began appearing in Dawson's area, arresting policy wheel operators. They weren't from the local stations, where Dawson handpicked the commanders and everybody else. They were being sent from downtown, as part of Kennelly's idea of reform. Kennelly had not sent in any building inspectors to lean on slum landlords, or done anything to raise the welfare limits, or opened job or housing opportunities to Negroes, but he was arresting their policy wheel operators.

Dawson visited him and explained that the nickel or dime a day a black person bet on policy was a needed diversion, much like the bingo in Catholic churches, the bets made by society people at the race tracks, and the gin games in the private clubs to which Kennelly belonged. "Our people can't afford to go to race tracks and private clubs, so they get a little pleasure out of policy," he told Kennelly.

Kennelly refused to call off the raids, and he was lofty about it, which was compounding his error. To Kennelly, Dawson was a mere politician, with a reputation for being avaricious, and he was black. Kennelly had as much respect for blacks as the next self-made white business-man living on the city's Gold Coast.

Dawson didn't ask again and he did not speak to Kennelly during the rest of the first term. He waited. His patience and closemouthedness had helped him become the most powerful black politician in America and a man who could deliver more Democratic votes than any one politician in Chicago. He controlled three wards.

He waited three years, until the party bosses got together to formalize Kennelly's candidacy for a second term.

After Chairman Gill went through the motions of saying that Kennelly was available again, and others went through the motions of extolling him, Horan said, "Shall we bring the mayor in? He is waiting outside."

At that moment, one of Dawson's lieutenants, who was sitting in for him, said, "The candidate is not acceptable to Congressman Dawson."

The committeemen, stunned, refused to believe Dawson's aide. They called Dawson in Washington and he calmly told them that it was true; he didn't want Kennelly.

They pleaded with him until he consented to come back to Chicago for a secret meeting with Kennelly to iron out their differences. The meeting took place a few days later in a hotel conference room. Kennelly sat behind a long table with some of the top ward leaders on either side. He sat a long time, flushed but silent, while Dawson limped back and forth on his artificial leg, cursing and shouting, blistering him for his coolness to the political chiefs in general, and his arrogance to Dawson in particular.

"Who do you think you are? I bring in the votes. I elect *you*. *You* are not needed, but the votes are needed. I deliver the votes to you, but you won't talk to *me*?"

When he finished, and Kennelly was humiliated, the others took him aside and Horan, an old friend, said: "Okay, you kicked his ass good. But we don't have another candidate." Dawson, who knew that in the beginning, agreed that Kennelly would get one more term, but only one.

That was the agreement among the party leaders, although Kennelly didn't know it. But Daley, one of the leaders, knew it, and he began planning accordingly. In 1953, after Kennelly was returned to office and Stevenson had his unfortunate encounter with Eisenhower, Gill resigned as chairman. Daley was to be elected by the committee. It was all set. Everybody had been persuaded, one way or another, and brought into line.

The Central Committee meeting began, but up popped the irrepressible South Siders, in the form of Ald. Clarence Wagner, who, despite his name, was Irish on his mother's side. Wagner called for a two-week postponement. That, of course, had not been in Daley's script. Gill granted the postponement, then everybody rushed off to find out what the South Side was up to.

The South Siders had decided that Alderman Wagner should be the next mayor, so they were going to nominate him for party chairman. The South Siders were tired of Kennelly and of outsiders like Senator Douglas and Stevenson. They viewed Daley as being closer to the new element than to his political and cultural heritage—namely, them.

Wagner, on the other hand, was one of them. He was finance chairman in the City Council, the number one chairmanship. Due to Kennelly's inactivity, Wagner was running much of city government from the council floor. He was, like most of the aldermen, a conservative, segregation-minded, and suspicious of the liberal newcomers.

Wagner was also a talented orator and lawyer, a tough political boss, and capable of giving Daley a fight he would remember.

The fight never developed. Two days after the surprise postponement, somebody got killed. This time it was Alderman Wagner, in an auto accident. The South Side rebellion ended, and in July 1953, Richard J. Daley, at the age of fifty-one, and thirty years after he rang his first doorbell as a lowly precinct captain, was elected chairman of the Cook County Democratic Central Committee.

He finally had his own machine.

Chapter IV

KUNSTLER: Mayor Daley, do you hold a position in the Cook County Democratic Committee?

WITNESS: I surely do, and I am proud of it. I am the leader of my party.

KUNSTLER: What was that?

WITNESS: I surely do, and I am very proud of it. I am the leader of the Democratic party in Cook County.

KUNSTLER: Your honor, I would like to strike from that answer anything about being very proud of it. I only asked whether he had a position in the Cook County Democratic party.

HOFFMAN: I will let the words "I surely do" stand. The words after those may go out and the jury may disregard the expression of the witness that he is very proud of his position.

The Hawk got his nickname because in his younger days he was the outside lookout man at a bookie joint. Then his eyes got weak, and he had to wear thick glasses, so he entered politics as a precinct worker.

He was a hustling precinct worker and brought out the vote, so he was rewarded with a patronage job. The Hawk, who had always loved uniforms but had never worn one, asked his ward committeeman if he could become a member of the county sheriff's police department. They gave him a uniform, badge, and gun, and declared him to be a policeman.

But the Hawk was afraid of firearms, so he asked if he could have a job that didn't require carrying a loaded gun. They put him inside the County Building, supervising the man who operated the freight elevator. He liked the job and did such a good job supervising the man who operated the freight elevator that the Hawk was promoted to sergeant.

When a Republican won the sheriff's office, the Hawk was out of work for one day before he turned up in the office of the county treasurer, wearing the uniform of a treasurer's guard. His new job was to sit at a table near the main entrance, beneath the big sign that said "County Treasurer," and when people came in and asked if they were in the county treasurer's office, the Hawk said that indeed they were. It was a good job, and he did it well, but it wasn't what he wanted because he really wasn't a policeman. Finally his committeeman arranged for him to become a member of the secretary of state's special force of highway inspectors, and he got to wear a uniform that had three colors and gold braid.

The Hawk is a tiny piece of the Machine. He is not necessarily a typical patronage worker, but he is not unusual. With about twenty-five thousand people owing their government jobs to political activity or influence, nothing is typical or unusual.

The Hawk keeps his job by getting out the Democratic vote in his precinct, paying monthly dues to the ward's coffers, buying and pushing tickets to his ward boss's golf outing and $25-a-plate dinners. His reward is a job that isn't difficult, hours that aren't demanding, and as long as he brings out the vote and the party keeps winning elections, he will remain employed. If he doesn't stay in the job he has, they will find something else for him.

Some precinct captains have had more jobs than they

can remember. Take Sam, who worked his first precinct forty-five years ago on the West Side.

"My first job was as a clerk over at the election board. In those days to succeed in politics you sometimes had to bash in a few heads. The Republicans in another ward heard about me and they brought me into one of their precincts where they were having trouble. I was brought in as a heavy, and I took care of the problem, so they got me a job in the state Department of Labor. The job was . . . uh . . . to tell the truth, I didn't do anything. I was a payroller. Then later I went to another ward as a Democratic precinct captain, where they were having a tough election. I did my job and I moved over to a job as a state policeman. Then later I was a city gas meter inspector, and a pipe fitter where they had to get me a union card, and an investigator for the attorney general, and when I retired I was an inspector in the Department of Weights and Measures."

The Hawk and Sam, as precinct captains, are basic parts of the Machine. There are some thirty-five hundred precincts in Chicago, and every one of them has a Democratic captain and most captains have assistant captains. They all have, or can have, jobs in government. The better the captain, the better the job. Many make upwards of fifteen thousand dollars a year as supervisors, inspectors, or minor department heads.

They aren't the lowest ranking members of the Machine. Below them are the people who swing mops in the public buildings, dump bedpans in the County Hospital, dig ditches, and perform other menial work. They don't work precincts regularly, although they help out at election time, but they do have to vote themselves and make sure their families vote, buy the usual tickets to political dinners, and in many wards, contribute about two percent of their salaries to the ward organization.

Above the precinct captain is that lordly figure the ward committeeman, known in local parlance as "the clout," "the Chinaman," "the guy," and "our beloved leader."

Vito Marzullo is a ward committeeman and an alderman. He was born in Italy and has an elementary school education, but for years when he arrived at political functions, a judge walked a few steps behind him, moving

ahead when there was a door to be opened. Marzullo had
put him on the bench. His ward, on the near Southwest
Side, is a pleasant stew of working class Italians, Poles,
Mexicans, and blacks. A short, erect, tough, and likable
man, he has had a Republican opponent only once in four
elections to the City Council. Marzullo has about four
hundred patronage jobs given to him by the Democratic
Central Committee to fill. He has more jobs than some
ward bosses because he has a stronger ward, with an
average turnout of something like 14,500 Democrats to
1,200 Republicans. But he has fewer jobs than some other
wards that are even stronger. Marzullo can tick off the jobs
he fills:

"I got an assistant state's attorney, and I got an assistant attorney general, I got an electrical inspector at twelve
thousand dollars a year, and I got street inspectors and
surveyors, and a county highway inspector. I got an administrative assistant to the zoning board and some people
in the secretary of state's office. I got fifty-nine precinct
captains and they all got assistants, and they all got good
jobs. The lawyers I got in jobs don't have to work precincts, but they have to come to my ward office and give
free legal advice to the people in the ward."

Service and favors, the staples of the precinct captain
and his ward boss. The service may be nothing more
than the ordinary municipal functions the citizen is paying taxes for. But there is always the feeling that they
could slip if the precinct captain wants them to, that the
garbage pickup might not be as good, that the dead tree
might not be cut down.

Service and favors. In earlier days, the captain could do
much more. The immigrant family looked to him as more
than a link with a new and strange government: he was
the government. He could tell them how to fill out their
papers, how to pay their taxes, how to get a license. He
was the welfare agency, with a basket of food and some
coal when things got tough, an entrée to the crowded
charity hospital. He could take care of it when one of the
kids got in trouble with the police. Social welfare agencies
and better times took away many of his functions, but
later there were still the traffic tickets to fix, the real
estate tax assessments he might lower. When a downtown

office didn't provide service, he was a direct link to government, somebody to cut through the bureaucracy.

In poor parts of the city, he has the added role of a threat. Don't vote, and you might lose your public housing apartment. Don't vote, and you might be cut off welfare. Don't vote, and you might have building inspectors poking around the house.

In the affluent areas, he is, sometimes, merely an errand boy, dropping off a tax bill on the way downtown, buying a vehicle sticker at City Hall, making sure that the streets are cleaned regularly, sounding out public opinion.

The payoff is on election day, when the votes are counted. If he produced, he is safe until the next election. If he didn't, that's it. "He has to go," Marzullo says. "If a company has a man who can't deliver, who can't sell the product, wouldn't he put somebody else in who can?"

Nobody except Chairman Daley knows precisely how many jobs the Machine controls. Some patronage jobs require special skills, so the jobholder doesn't have to do political work. Some are under civil service. And when the Republicans occasionally win a county office, the jobs change hands. There were more patronage jobs under the old Kelly-Nash Machine of the thirties and forties, but civil service reform efforts hurt the Machine. Some of the damage has been undone by Daley, however, who let civil service jobs slip back into patronage by giving tests infrequently or making them so difficult that few can pass, thus making it necessary to hire "temporary" employees, who stay "temporary" for the rest of their lives. Even civil service employees are subject to political pressures in the form of unwanted transfers, withheld promotions.

On certain special occasions, it is possible to see much of the Machine's patronage army assembled and marching. The annual St. Patrick's Day parade down State Street, with Daley leading the way, is a display of might that knots the stomachs of Republicans. An even more remarkable display of patronage power is seen at the State Fair, when on "Democrat Day" thousands of city workers are loaded into buses, trains, and cars which converge on the fairgrounds outside Springfield. The highlight of the fair is when Daley proudly hoofs down the middle of the grounds' dusty racetrack in ninety-degree heat with thousands of his sweating but devoted workers tramping behind him, wearing old-fashioned straw hats and derbies. The Illinois attorney general's staff of lawyers once thrilled the rustics with a crack manual of arms performance, using Daley placards instead of rifles.

Another reason the size of the patronage army is impossible to measure is that it extends beyond the twenty to twenty-five thousand government jobs. The Machine has jobs at racetracks, public utilities, private industry, and the Chicago Transit Authority, which is the bus and subway system, and will help arrange easy union cards.

Out of the ranks of the patronage workers rise the Marzullos, fifty ward committeemen who, with thirty suburban township committeemen, sit as the Central Committee. For them the reward is more than a comfortable payroll job. If they don't prosper, it is because they are ignoring the advice of their Tammany cousin George Washington Plunkett, who said, "I seen my opportunities and I took 'em." Chicago's ward bosses take 'em, too.

Most of them hold an elective office. Many of the Daley aldermen are ward bosses. Several are county commissioners. Others hold office as county clerk, assessor, or recorder of deeds and a few are congressmen and state legislators. Those who don't hold office are given top jobs running city departments, whether they know anything about the work or not. A ward boss who was given a $28,000-a-year job as head of the city's huge sewer system was asked what his experience was. "About twenty years ago I was a house drain inspector." "Did you ever work in the sewers?" "No, but many a time I lifted a lid to see if they were flowing." "Do you have an engineering background?" "Sort of. I took some independent courses at a school I forget the name of, and in 1932 I was a plumber's helper." His background was adequate: his ward usually carries by fifteen thousand to three thousand votes.

The elective offices and jobs provide the status, identity, and retinue of coat holders and door openers, but financially only the household money. About a third of them are lawyers, and the clients leap at them. Most of the judges came up through the Machine; many are former ward bosses themselves. This doesn't mean cases are always rigged, but one cannot underestimate the power of

sentimentality. The political lawyers are greatly in demand for zoning disputes, big real estate ventures, and
anything else that brings a company into contact with city
agencies. When a New York corporation decided to bid
for a lucrative Chicago cable TV franchise, they promptly
tried to retain the former head of the city's legal department to represent them.

Those who don't have the advantage of a law degree
turn to the old reliable, insurance. To be a success in the
insurance field, a ward boss needs only two things: an
office with his name on it and somebody in the office who
knows how to write policies. All stores and businesses
need insurance. Why not force the premium on the friendly
ward boss? As Marzullo says, everybody needs favors.

One of the most successful political insurance firms is
operated by party ancient Joe Gill. Gill gets a big slice of
the city's insurance on public properties, like the Civic
Center and O'Hare Airport. There are no negotiations or
competitive bidding. The policies are given to him because
he is Joe Gill. How many votes does Prudential Life
deliver? The city's premiums are about $500,000 a year,
giving Gill's firm a yearly profit of as much as $100,000.

Another firm, founded by the late Al Horan, and later
operated by his heirs and County Assessor P. J. Cullerton,
gets $100,000 a year in premiums from the city's park
district. Since Cullerton is the man who sets the taxable
value of all property in Cook County, it is likely that some
big property owners would feel more secure being pro-
tected by his insurance.

When the city's sprawling lake front convention hall was
built, the insurance business was tossed at the insurance
firm founded by George Dunne, a ward boss and County
Board president.

Another old-line firm is operated by John D'Arco, the
crime syndicate's man in the Central Committee. He rep-
resents the First Ward, which includes the Loop, a gold-
mine of insurable property. D'Arco has never bothered to
deny that he is a political appendage of the Mafia, probably because he knows that nobody would believe him. A
denial would sound strained in light of his bad habit of
being seen with Mafia bosses in public. Besides, the First

Ward was controlled by the Mafia long before D'Arco became alderman and ward committeeman.

D'Arco's presence in the Central Committee has sometimes been an embarrassment to Chairman Daley. Despite D'Arco's understandable efforts to be discreet, he can't avoid personal publicity because the FBI is always following the people with whom he associates. When D'Arco announced that he was leaving the City Council because of poor health, while remaining ward committeeman, the FBI leaked the fact that Mafia chief Sam Giancana had ordered him out of the council in a pique over something or other. Giancana could do that, because it is his ward; D'Arco only watches it for him. One of Giancana's relatives has turned up as an aide to a First Ward congressman. Another Giancana relative was elected to the state Senate. At Daley's urging, the First Ward organization made an effort to improve its image by running a young banker for alderman. But the banker finally resigned from the council, saying that being the First Ward's alderman was ruining his reputation.

When he is asked about the First Ward, Daley retreats to the democratic position that the people elect D'Arco and their other representatives, and who is he to argue with the people? He has the authority, as party chairman, to strip the First Ward, or any ward, of its patronage, and there are times when he surely must want to do so. Raids on Syndicate gambling houses sometimes turn up city workers, usually sponsored by the First Ward organization. While he has the authority to take away the jobs, it would cause delight in the press and put him in the position of confirming the Mafia's participation in the Machine. He prefers to suffer quietly through the periodic flaps.

The question is often raised whether he actually has the power, in addition to the authority, to politically disable the Mafia. It has been in city government longer than he has, and has graduated its political lackeys to judgeships, the various legislative bodies, and positions throughout government. While it no longer is the controlling force it was in Thompson's administration, or as arrogantly obvious as it was under Kelly-Nash, it remains a part of the Machine, and so long as it doesn't challenge him but is satisfied with its limited share, Daley can live with it, just as he lives with the rascals in Springfield.

Ward bosses are men of ambition, so when they aren't busy with politics or their outside professions, they are on the alert for "deals." At any given moment, a group of them, and their followers, are either planning a deal, hatching a deal, or looking for a deal.

Assessor Cullerton and a circle of his friends have gone in for buying up stretches of exurban land for golf courses, resorts, and the like. Others hold interests in racetracks, which depend on political goodwill for additional racing dates.

The city's dramatic physical redevelopment has been a boon to the political world as well as the private investors. There are so many deals involving ranking members of the Machine that it has been suggested that the city slogan be changed from *Urbs In Horto,* which means "City in a Garden," to *Ubi Est Mea,* which means "Where's mine?"

From where Daley sits, alone atop the Machine, he sees all the parts, and his job is to keep them functioning properly. One part that has been brought into perfect synchronization is organized labor—perhaps the single biggest factor in the unique survival of the big city organization in Chicago. Labor provides Daley with his strongest personal support and contributes great sums to his campaigns. Daley's roots are deep in organized labor. His father was an organizer of his sheet-metal workers' local, and Bridgeport was always a union neighborhood. With politics and the priesthood, union activity was one of the more heavily traveled roads to success. Daley grew up with Steve Bailey, who became head of the Plumbers' Union, and as Daley developed politically, Bailey brought him into contact with other labor leaders.

Thousands of trade union men are employed by local government. Unlike the federal government and many other cities, Chicago always pays the top construction rate, rather than the lower maintenance scale, although most of the work is maintenance. Daley's massive public works projects, gilded with overtime pay in his rush to cut ribbons before elections, are another major source of union jobs.

His policy is that a labor leader be appointed to every

policy-making city board or committee. In recent years, it has worked out this way: the head of the Janitors' Union was on the police board, the park board, the Public Buildings Commission, and several others. The head of the Plumbers' Union was on the Board of Health and ran the St. Patrick's Day parade. The head of the Electricians' Union was vice-president of the Board of Education. The Clothing Workers' Union had a man on the library board. The Municipal Employees' Union boss was on the Chicago Housing Authority, which runs the city's public housing projects. The head of the Chicago Federation of Labor and somebody from the Teamsters' Union were helping run the poverty program. And the sons of union officials find the door to City Hall open if they decide on a career in politics.

The third major part of the Machine is money. Once again, only Daley knows how much it has and how it is spent. As party chairman, he controls its treasury. The spending is lavish. Even when running against a listless nobody, Daley may spend a million dollars. The amount used for "precinct money," which is handed out to the precinct captains and used in any way that helps bring out the Democratic vote, can exceed the entire Republican campaign outlay. This can mean paying out a couple of dollars or a couple of chickens to voters in poor neighborhoods, or bottles of cheap wine in the Skid Row areas. Republicans claim that the Democrats will spend as much as $300,000 in precinct money alone for a city election. To retain a crucial office, such as that of county assessor, hundreds of thousands have been spent on billboard advertising alone. Add to that the TV and radio saturation, and the spending for local campaigning exceeds by far the cost-per-vote level of national campaigning.

The money comes from countless sources. From the patronage army, it goes into the ward offices as dues, and part of it is turned over to party headquarters. Every ward leader throws his annual $25-a-head golf days, corned beef dinners, and picnics. The ticket books are thrust at the patronage workers and they either sell them or, as they say, "eat them," bearing the cost themselves.

There are "ward books," with page after page of advertising, sold by precinct workers to local businesses and other favorseekers. Alderman Marzullo puts out a 350-page ad book every year, at one hundred dollars a page. There are no blank pages in his book. The ward organizations keep what they need to function, and the rest is funneled to party headquarters.

Contractors may be the biggest of all contributors. Daley's public works program has poured billions into their pockets, and they in turn have given millions back to the party in contributions. Much of it comes from contractors who are favored, despite the seemingly fair system of competitive bidding. In some fields, only a handful of contractors ever bid, and they manage to arrange things so that at the end of the year each has received about the same amount of work and the same profit. A contractor who is not part of this "brotherhood" refrains from bidding on governmental work. If he tries to push his way in by submitting a reasonable bid, which would assure him of being the successful low bidder, he may suddenly find that the unions are unable to supply him with the workers he needs.

Even Republican businessmen contribute money to the Machine, more than they give to Republican candidates. Republicans can't do anything for them, but Daley can.

The Machine's vast resources have made it nearly impossible for Republicans to offer more than a fluttering fight in city elections. Daley, to flaunt his strength and to keep his organization in trim, will crank out four hundred thousand primary votes for himself running unopposed. His opponent will be lucky to get seventy thousand Republicans interested enough to cast a primary vote.

Unlike New York, Los Angeles, and other major cities, Chicago has no independent parties or candidates jumping in to threaten, or at least pull votes away from the leaders. It is no accident. Illinois election laws are stacked against an independent's ever getting his name on a voting machine.

In New York, a regular party candidate needs five thousand signatures on his nominating petitions, and an independent must have seventy-five hundred. With any kind of volunteer organization, an independent can get the names, which is why New York will have half a dozen candidates for mayor.

The requirements are even less demanding in L.A., where a candidate needs a seven-hundred-dollar filing fee and petitions bearing five hundred names. L.A. voters have a dozen or so candidates from which to choose.

But Chicago has never, in this century, had more than two candidates for the office of mayor. The state legislature took care of the threat from troublesome independents years ago.

When Daley files his nominating petitions, he needs about thirty-nine hundred names, a figure based on one-half of one percent of his party's vote in the previous election. Daley usually gets so many names that the petitions have to be brought in by truck. Using the same formula his Republican opponent needs about twenty-five hundred signatures, which isn't difficult, even for a Chicago Republican.

But an independent would have to bring in about sixty to seventy thousand signatures. He needs five percent of the previous total vote cast. And not just anybody's signature: only legally defined independents, those who have not voted in the recent partisan primaries.

That's why there are only two candidates for mayor and the other offices in Chicago—a Republican and a Democrat. And sometimes there aren't even that many, Mayor Kelly having once handpicked his Republican opponent.

The only alternative for an independent is to run as a write-in candidate, a waste of time.

It has never happened, but if an independent somehow managed to build an organization big and enthusiastic enough to find seventy thousand independent voters who would sign his petition, he would probably need an extra thirty thousand signatures to be sure of getting past the Chicago Election Board, which runs the city's elections and rules on the validity of nominating petitions. Names can be ruled invalid for anything short of failing to dot an "i." An illiterate's "X" might be acceptable on a Machine candidate's petition, but the Election Board is meticulous about those of anybody else.

The board used to be run by a frank old rogue, Sidney

Holzman, who summed up its attitude toward the aspirations of independents, Republicans, and other foreigners:

"We throw their petitions up to the ceiling, and those that stick are good."

Despite all these safeguards and its lopsided superiority over local opposition, the Machine never fails to run scared. For this reason, or maybe out of habit, it never misses a chance to steal a certain number of votes and trample all over the voting laws. Most of it goes on in the wards where the voters are lower middle class, black, poor white, or on the bottle. To assure party loyalty, the precinct captains merely accompany the voter into the voting machine. They aren't supposed to be sticking their heads in, but that's the only way they can be sure the person votes Democratic. They get away with it because the election judges, who are citizens hired to supervise each polling place, don't protest. The Democratic election judges don't mind, and the Republican election judges are probably Democrats. The Republicans assign poll watchers to combat fraud but they never have enough people to cover all of the precincts. If they prevented the common practices, imaginative precinct captains would merely turn to others. In some wards, politically obligated doctors sign stacks of blank affidavits, attesting to the illness of people they have never seen, thus permitting the precinct captain to vote the people in their homes as absentee voters for reasons of illness. And several investigations have established that death does not always keep a person's vote from being cast.

The aforementioned Holzman was always philosophical about vote fraud, conceding that it occurred, and even saying that "a good precinct captain will always find a way to steal votes," but asserting: "In city elections, we don't have to steal to win. And in state-wide elections, the Republicans are stealing so much downstate, that all we do is balance it out."

Out of this vast amalgam of patronage, money, special interests, restrictive election laws, and organizational discipline emerge a handful of candidates, and they are what it is supposed to be all about.

Most of them come up through the system, as Daley did, beginning as doorbell ringers, working in the jobs their sponsors got for them, pushing the ward book, buying the tickets, doing the favors, holding the coats, opening the doors, putting in the fix, and inching their way up to the organizational ladder, waiting for somebody to die and the chance to go to the legislature, into the City Council, and maybe someday something even bigger.

As hard as a party member may try, and as bright and presentable as he may be, he probably won't make it if he isn't from a strong ward with an influential ward boss. A loyal, hard-working City Hall lawyer can become a judge, if his ward brings in the vote and his sponsor pushes him, while in another ward, where the Republicans dominate and the ward boss just hangs on, the City Hall lawyer can only dream of his black robe.

Judge Wexler, Daley's night school classmate, lived with this problem. Wexler had worked feverishly as the city's chief prosecutor of slum cases, dragging landlords into court, reaping publicity for the mayor's administration, while deftly avoiding the toes of slum landlords who had political connections. For years he trotted into Daley's office with his news clippings. But when slate-making time came around, other people got to be judges.

"My ward committeeman was so weak, he couldn't do anything. I used to ask him for a letter to the Central Committee sponsoring me for a judgeship. You have to have a sponsoring letter. And he'd say: 'A letter for you? I want to be a judge myself, and I'm not getting anywhere.' I would have never made it if it hadn't been for Daley and knowing him from night school. He did it for me personally."

Wexler was fortunate. For the others with ambitions, it is either a strong committeeman and advancement, or an obscure job with nothing to put in the scrap book.

Only one other shortcut exists, and it is part of the system of the Machine: nepotism. A Chicago Rip Van Winkle could awaken to the political news columns and, reading the names, think that time had stood still.

There was Otto Kerner, Cermak's confidante and a federal judge, and he begat Otto Kerner, governor, federal judge, and husband of Cermak's daughter; John Clark, ward boss and assessor, begat William Clark, attorney general and 1968 U.S. Senate candidate; Adlai Stevenson, governor and presidential candidate, begat Adlai Stevenson, U.S. Senator; Dan Ryan, ward boss and County Board president, begat Dan Ryan, ward boss and County Board president; Edward Dunne, mayor, begat Robert Jerome Dunne, judge; John J. Touhy, ward boss and holder of many offices, begat John M. Touhy, Illinois House Speaker; Joe Rostenkowski, ward boss, begat Daniel Rostenkowski, congressman; Arthur Elrod, ward boss and county commissioner, begat Richard Elrod, sheriff; John Toman, ward boss and sheriff, begat Andrew Toman, county coroner; Thomas Keane, ward boss and alderman, begat Thomas Keane, ward boss and alderman; Joe Burke, ward boss and alderman, begat Edward Burke, ward boss and alderman; Paul Sheridan, ward boss and alderman, begat Paul Sheridan, alderman; Theodore Swinarski, ward boss, begat Donald Swinarski, alderman; Ald. David Hartigan begat Neil Hartigan, ward boss and chief park district attorney; Louis Garippo, ward boss, begat Louis Garippo, judge; Michael Igoe, federal judge, begat Michael Igoe, County Board secretary; Daniel McNamara, union leader, begat Daniel McNamara, judge; Thomas Murray, union leader and school board member, begat James Murray, congressman and alderman; Peter Shannon, businessman and friend of Daley, begat Dan Shannon, Park District president; Morgan Murphy, Sr., business executive and friend of Daley, begat Morgan Murphy, Jr., congressman; William Downes, real estate expert and friend of Daley, begat a daughter, who married a young man named David Stahl, who became deputy mayor; James Conlisk, police captain and City Hall favorite, begat James Conlisk, police superintendent; Daniel Coman, ward boss and city forestry chief, begat Daniel Coman, head of the state's attorney's civil division.

They are their brothers' keepers, too.

Alderman Keane keeps his brother on the powerful board of real estate tax appeals; Assessor Cullerton keeps his brother in the City Council and his brother-in-law as his chief deputy assessor; Ald. Harry Sain kept his brother as city jail warden when sheriff; and County Board President Dunne keeps his brother as boss of O'Hare and Midway airports, and Cong. John Kluczynski keeps his brother on the state Supreme Court.

Nobody in the Machine is more family conscious than Chairman Daley. Cousin John Daley became a ward committeeman and served several terms in the state legislature, where his remarkable resemblance to the mayor sometimes unnerved his associates. Uncle Martin Daley had a well paying job in county government that he did so skillfully he seldom had to leave his home. Cousin Richard Curry heads the city's legal department. Daley's four sons are just finishing law school, so their public careers have not yet been launched, but the eldest, Richard, at twenty-seven, was a candidate for delegate from his district to the state constitutional convention. He piled up the biggest vote in the state. The people in Bridgeport recognize talent. And the sons have been judge's clerks while going through school. When one of the mayor's daughters married, Daley promptly found a city executive job for the father of his new son-in-law.

Daley didn't come from a big family but he married into one, and so Eleanor Guilfoyle's parents might well have said that they did not lose a daughter, they gained an employment agency. Mrs. Daley's nephew has been in several key jobs. Her sister's husband became a police captain. A brother is an engineer in the school system. Stories about the number of Guilfoyles, and cousins and in-laws of Guilfoyles, in the patronage army have taken on legendary tones.

There are exceptions to the rules of party apprenticeship and nepotism. A few independent Democrats have been dogged enough to defeat weak Machine candidates in primaries for alderman, or, as happened once in the Daley years, for a seat in Congress. But it is never easy, and the strain leaves most independents so exhausted that most of them eventually embrace the Machine, at least gently, to avoid recurring primary struggles.

In theory, anybody can walk right into party headquarters at slate-making time, go before the ward bosses who make up the committee, and present themselves as prospective candidates. One political hanger-on, a disc jockey, even caught them in a mirthful mood, and when he actually got down on his knees and begged, they let him

run for a minor office. But even the slate-makers do not
kid themselves into thinking they are deciding who the candidates will be. They listen to the applicants, push their
favorites, the men from their wards, and wait for Chairman Daley to make up his mind. Some of the men on
the slate-making committee have been surprised to find
that they themselves were slated to run for offices they
hadn't even sought. It is a one-man show, and they know
it. This vignette illustrates it:

In 1968, slate-makers were putting together their county
ticket. They listened to the applicants, talked it over, then
Daley and a couple of the party ancients came out of
another room with the list.

Daley had decided that the strongest candidate for the
crucial office of state's attorney, the county's prosecutor,
would be Edward Hanrahan, a former federal prosecutor.
It is a "must" office because a Republican would use it to
investigate City Hall. Hanrahan was the strongest candidate because his Republican opponent also had an Irish
name.

But slating Hanrahan required that the incumbent, John
Stamos, who had been appointed to fill a vacancy, be
shifted to something else. Stamos, a diligent and skilled
young prosecutor, was Greek; Greeks were a small voting
bloc, and Stamos was just professional and aloof enough
to make some party elders nervous. Daley had decided
to let Stamos run for the office of Illinois attorney general, which has prestige but less power and challenge.
That completed the ticket.

Their decision made for them, the slate-makers filed
out of the conference room to go downstairs and meet the
news media. As they came out, one of them saw Stamos
and said, "Congratulations, John, you're going for attorney
general."

"Bullshit," Stamos said, adding, "I won't go for it."
Daley reasoned, but Stamos repeated, "Bullshit." And left
the hotel.

While the slate-makers stood around looking confused, Daley told a secretary to call Frank Lorenz, an
obedient party regular who was between elective offices.
She got him on the phone and Daley said, "Come on
over, Frank, you're the candidate for attorney general."

One of the slate-makers later said: "If Lorenz had stepped out to take a piss, he would have missed out, and the next guy Daley thought of would have got it, if he answered his phone. That's the way things are run sometimes, and everybody says we're so goddamn well organized."

A minute or two later, it was all resolved. Normally, Stamos would have been punished. But for party unity and to avoid alienating big Greek financial contributors, he was elevated to the state appellate court.

"You never know what in the hell is going to happen in there," a ward boss said. "He moves us around like a bunch of chess pieces. He knows why he's doing it because he's like a Russian with a ten-year plan, but we never know. I think his idea is to slate people who aren't going to try to rival him or add to someone else's strength. Look at how Cullerton got to be assessor. First he was a nothing alderman. He was a real nothing. But Daley put him in as finance chairman so he could have somebody who wouldn't get out of line. Then he put him in as assessor. Keane wanted assessor for his brother George. George would have loved it. Funny how people love to be assessor, haw! But Daley wasn't about to give Tom Keane the assessor's office, so he looked around and there was faithful Parky Cullerton.

"When he had to pick a chief judge, who were the logical guys? Neil Harrington, but he couldn't give it to Neil because he used to be part of the old South Side action, and Daley wouldn't trust him. Harold Ward? He is independent, he might tell Daley to go screw himself or something.

"So he gave it to John Boyle, because he knew he'd have Boyle's complete loyalty. Why? Because Boyle had that scandal when he was state's attorney years ago and after that he couldn't get elected dogcatcher. He was a whipped dog, so he was perfect for Daley.

"And there's this thing he has with old people. Jesus, we've reslated people who were so senile they didn't even know what office they were running for. When it gets to that point, you know it has got to be something more than him being softhearted. There were some we could have just told them they were being reslated, and they would never have known the difference. He does it because then he doesn't have to worry about them. They'll sit there on the County Board or wherever they are and do just what they're told.

"It's one-man rule, absolutely. It used to be that if Kelly got mad at you, there were seven or eight guys you could go to and get it squared. The same thing with Nash, and when Arvey was chairman. But there's only one Daley. You're dead if he doesn't like you. There's no point in going to someone to try to get it squared because they can't, and they won't even try because they're afraid it'll get him mad at them. He's a friend of mine, but he can be a mean prick."

Just how mean, and how subtle, was discovered by Arnold Maremont, a millionaire industrialist and art collector who decided he wanted to go into politics and to start at the top.

Daley does not dislike millionaires. He lets them contribute to the party, serve on advisory boards, take on time-consuming appointments, and help elect Machine Democrats to office.

Maremont had done it all. He contribtued money, worked in Governor Kerner's campaign, led a campaign to pass a $150,000,000 bond issue that revitalized the state's mental health program, and pitched in on numerous liberal causes and mental health and welfare programs.

His dream was to be a U.S. senator, and in early 1961 he went to Daley's office and told him that he'd like to run against Sen. Everett Dirksen. He made it clear that he wanted to do it properly and not jump into the primary as a maverick. The party's blessing was what he was after.

Daley showed interest, but said he had certain reservations: mainly he wasn't sure if downstate county chairmen would support a Jew. He suggested that Maremont tour the state, talk to the county chairmen, and he indicated strongly that if Maremont made a good showing, he'd be Daley's man.

Maremont pushed aside his business and civic work and spent most of the early summer barnstorming through Illinois. A spunky, brash man, he'd walk into a bar in a tiny Southern Illinois town—grits and gravy country—and announce: "My name's Arnold Maremont. I want to run for the Senate and I'm a Jew." People seemed to like him, as he wolfed down chicken and peas dinners at the county meetings, charming little old ladies and picking up support from the chairmen.

All the while, he sent back regular reports to Daley: they will go for a Jew! Elated, he headed back to Chicago, ready to give Daley his final report and the good news. He got back to town just in time to pick up that day's papers and read that Daley had, indeed, decided to slate a Jewish senatorial candidate: Cong. Sidney Yates, a party regular.

That ended Maremont's political ambitions. Furious, he was convinced that Daley had merely used him to conduct a free one-man survey of downstate Illinois. He wouldn't have even tried had he ever heard Daley explain why he is so dedicated a party man: "The party permits ordinary people to get ahead. Without the party, I couldn't be mayor. The rich guys can get elected on their money, but somebody like me, an ordinary person, needs the party. Without the party, only the rich would be elected to office."

If Daley's one-man rule bothers the men who sit on the Central Committee, they are careful to keep it to themselves. The meetings take on the mood of a religious service, with the committeemen chanting their praise of his leadership. "It has been . . . my pleasure and honor . . . to give him my advice. . . . The greatest mayor . . . in the country . . . the world . . . the history of the world . . ."

Only once in recent years has anybody stood up and talked back, and he was one of the suburban committeemen, generally referred to around party headquarters as "a bunch of meatheads."

The suburban committeeman, Lynn Williams, a wealthy manufacturer and probably the most liberal member of the Central Committee, had been angered by Daley's attacks on liberals after the 1968 Democratic Convention. Daley had been making speeches lambasting pseudoliberals, liberal-intellectuals, suburban liberals, suburban liberal-intellectuals, and pseudoliberal-intellectual suburbanites. He had been shouting: "Who in the hell do those people think they are? Who are they to tell us how to run our party?"

Williams, a strong supporter of young Adlai Stevenson, who had angered Daley with an attack on "feudal" politics, stood up, finally, at a Central Committee meeting and delivered a scathing rebuttal to Daley, saying that without liberal participation the party would be nothing but a skeleton, its only goal, power.

As he talked, the committeemen's heads swiveled as if they were watching a tennis game, wonder and fear on their faces. They had never heard such talk, and wondered what Chairman Daley would do. Strike him with lightning. Throw the bum out?

When Williams finished, Daley, in a surprisingly soft voice, said, "I've always been a liberal myself."

Other committeemen joined in his defense, recalling countless liberal acts by Daley. One man shouted at Williams, "Perhaps you didn't know, but this happens to be a very liberal outfit."

The shock of the committeemen at the sound of somebody criticizing Daley didn't surprise Williams. He has said: "Most of them are mediocrities at best, and not very intelligent. The more successful demonstrate cunning. Most are in need of slavery—their own—and they want to follow a strong leader."

In March 1970, the committeemen met for the purpose of reelecting Daley chairman. Alderman Keane nominated him and eighteen other committeemen made lengthy speeches seconding the nomination. One of them recited, "R, you're rare; I, you're important; C, you're courageous; H, you're heavenly; A, you're able; R, you're renowned; D, you're Democratic; J, is for your being a joy to know; D, you're diligent; A, you're adorable; L, you're loyal; E, you're energetic; and Y, you're youthful."

Once again Lynn Williams stood, but not to criticize. He, too, joined in the praise and made one of the seconding speeches. Daley had since slated young Adlai Stevenson III, whom Williams had supported, for the U.S. Senate. Daley and Williams even exchanged handshakes. In a way, Williams seemed to emphasize his own point about the committee's need to follow a strong leader.

Chapter V

KUNSTLER: Mayor Daley, there is an organization, an entity, called the Park District, is there not?

WITNESS: Yes, there is.

KUNSTLER: What is the title of the person who is chief officer of the Park District?

WITNESS: The president is the chief officer. . . .The president is William McFetridge.

KUNSTLER: Now, prior to the opening of the Democratic National Convention in 1968, did you have occasion, let's say between March and August, to meet with Mr. McFetridge. . . .

WITNESS: I would talk to him occasionally. There was no set meeting, but we would always meet at least once or twice a month and discuss problems of the Park District.

KUNSTLER: In those discussions, did you ever have occasion to discuss the issuance of permits. . . .

WITNESS: I gave him the same instructions I give every department . . . to cooperate . . . to be as helpful as possible.

KUNSTLER: . . . Is that the same William McFetridge who announced your candidacy as mayor in 1955?

FORAN: Objection.

The time had come for Martin Kennelly to go. He had served his purpose, allowing himself to be used as a front man to save the Machine from extinction, and it, in return, had given him eight glory-filled years, all the banquets he could sit through, all the ribbons he could cut. Now, in 1955, it was time for him to return that which was theirs, the power of the office on five.

They let him know how things stood as delicately as they knew how. They stopped talking to him, which is always a hint that something is up. They stopped asking him to come out to their political rallies. To make sure the message was getting through, they leaked stories to the press that Daley was going to be the candidate. But nothing fazed Kennelly. He sat in his office looking confident and relaxed. They had turned out most of the lights, put out the cat, the wife had gone to bed, his glass was empty and there was no refill, and the host was yawning in his face. But Kennelly sat and smiled. One of his aides later said:

"Martin thought that he'd get another term. He was sure that when he went into the committee and talked to them, he'd con them and charm them, and that they wouldn't have the guts to dump him. He figured the people were behind him and that they'd be afraid of a primary fight. There was never any doubt in his mind that when he got in there, he'd convince them one way or another that he was their man."

To let the Machine know how he stood, Kennelly jumped the gun on them, allowing the Citizens to Reelect Kennelly to open campaign headquarters in the Loop a week before the slate-makers began their hearings. He sent a telegram to Chairman Daley, inviting him to the opening, a customary appearance for the party chairman, and gave copies of the message to the press.

Daley sent his answer, an inspired rebuff: "I promised to take my children to see Santa Claus that day." Then he appointed the ward bosses who would sit as the slate-making committee. All were loyal to him. Any other kind would have been hard to find.

On December 14, Kennelly walked over to party headquarters in the Morrison Hotel and went into the meeting room. He was surprised to see Daley, who wasn't on the committee, sitting on the end of the long table, his arms crossed, expressionless. Kennelly read a six-paragraph statement outlining the accomplishments of his administration and stating his desire to be endorsed for a third term. Then he put it in his coat pocket and sat back to answer questions and engage in the usual informal talk session. This was where he would get them.

Nobody said anything. Several seconds passed. Kennelly shifted around in his chair and finally had to ask, "Do you have any questions?" The heads shook. Some looked away. Then the committee chairman said, "Thank you Mr. Mayor." That was it. Three minutes and fifty-six seconds after he walked in, full of confidence, Kennelly was going down the hotel corridor, his face quite pale.

A few days later the slate-makers finished their hearings, rounded out the city ticket, and announced that they had "drafted" Daley as their candidate for mayor. Alderman Tom Keane, who would spend the rest of his career waiting for his chance, recalls the "draft." "I guess we wanted him. That was part of it. But he wanted it and he went after it. You don't get drafted for an office. Ha! You don't sit around waiting to be anointed. You go after it, and he wanted it more than anybody else did, and he worked at getting it, and that's how he got it. I don't think he had originally set his goal specifically at becoming mayor. He would have gone for governor or anything else. He wanted power and an office."

Daley accepted the draft and promptly made promises. "There will be no sabotage of the civil service program during my administration. The man who heads the Police Department will be given real authority. His office will not be in City Hall, but in the Central Police Headquarters, where the commissioner of police belongs." Later, Daley would shrink civil service and expand the patronage army. And the police chief would stay right in City Hall, bowing to political pressures.

Kennelly raged to the press about the evil party bosses and they took up his cry. The editorial writers decided that Daley wasn't a new-breed, progressive political leader after all. They changed ribbons and wrote him back into "boss" status, a tool of the Machine.

Kennelly announced that he wouldn't be dumped. He

would enter the primary and beat the Machine in the February voting. It had been done before. A popular Polish judge had fought the Machine's efforts to unseat him, and had won by six thousand votes. And that had happened only seventeen years earlier.

With the support of the press, which preferred simple issues, Kennelly knew that his only chance was to hammer away at one theme: goodness, decency, and honesty against the clutching hands of the ward bosses. Since Daley's leading backers were people like Al Horan, Tom Keane, and Bill Dawson, it wasn't a difficult proposition to sell.

Kennelly's support came from the press, business, a few small unions, and, surprisingly, from two ward bosses. One of them, Tom Nash, the old Capone gang lawyer, was the last of the unreconstructed South Side rebels. It wasn't that he liked Kennelly—he was still mad at Daley for siding with Kelly years earlier. More important was the backing of Frank Keenan, the county assessor and a far North Side ward boss. Keenan was ambitious and didn't like seeing Daley taking over, so he became Kennelly's campaign manager. As assessor, he also persuaded big property owners to contribute to the Kennelly campaign fund.

One would think that with forty-eight ward committeemen behind him, a man would be big enough to suffer through the loss of two. But Daley was furious, especially at Keenan, and set out to get revenge immediately. He went to Dan Ryan, president of the County Board, and demanded that the board cut the assessor's budget, which would bring chaos to Keenan's office. Ryan refused, but Daley persisted, so Ryan, whose family had been politically powerful when Daley was ringing doorbells, said: "I'm president of the board and I'm running my own show. I'm not going to take your heat. I'd have the civic federation and everybody else on my neck for doing something like that." The two of them shouted at each other and until Daley stomped out, the secretaries feared they would come to blows. Daley would have to live with only forty-eight committeemen on his side.

Kennelly's campaign strategy, as Keenan explained it to him, was to offset the vote in the strong Machine wards with a huge protest vote in the outlying residential wards, where the precinct captain's influence was minimal. The only flaw in that plan was that the outlying wards were where the Republicans had their greatest strength, and persuading them to vote in a Democratic primary, requiring public declaration of their party preference, would be a neat trick.

Daley's campaign wasn't based on any such ifs. The ward bosses and precinct captains knew their jobs. They would work even harder than usual, because when Kennelly warned that Daley would kill civil service and open up the town, the precinct captains believed him, and the prospect inspired them.

The big unions came through for Daley, with William McFetridge of the Janitors' Union leading the way. They admitted to contributing a minimum of $215,000 for the primary and regular elections, an impressive sum for a city contest. They also brought in sound trucks, extra precinct workers, and printed more than a half million pieces of campaign literature.

In the middle of the primary fight was a third candidate, Benjamin Adamowski, the one man in the party who was as ambitious as Daley. A fine orator, and just as straight-laced as Daley, Adamowski had grown more and more resentful as Daley climbed past him. He had been a political boy wonder when Daley first came to the legislature, and his ambition was to become the city's first Polish-American mayor. He knew that if Daley took over, he could forget his dream, so he entered the primary without hopes of winning, but with the intention of pulling some of the Polish-American vote, the largest ethnic bloc in the city, away from the Machine.

The Machine is at its best in primaries, but Daley was taking no chances. He made sure that his name would appear above Kennelly's on the voting machines and ballots. This is considered an advantage, since politicians assume that a certain number of voters are so stupid that they vote for the first name they see. Kennelly also wanted this position. So they had a race for it.

The top spot goes to the candidate whose petitions are filed first with the city clerk. On the first day for filing petitions, Kennelly's men were waiting outside the city clerk's office before it opened, watching for the mail to arrive with his petitions. The mail bag came, a city employee opened the clerk's office and carried the bag inside, stamped it "8:18 A.M.," dumped the contents out, and there were Kennelly's petitions. His men smiled.

Just then, somebody noticed another mail bag, outside the private office of the city clerk. It has been brought in the back door, while the front door was still locked, and was stamped "8:13 A.M." In it were Daley's petitions. Kennelly's men protested, but there are no laws against mail coming in the back door.

The campaigns began, with Kennelly leaning heavily on radio and television, charging Daley with bossism. Daley leaned heavily on his precinct captains, charging Kennelly with inactivity. On February 22, Dawson and the others cracked the whip and the vote poured out. The blacks went in, pulled the lever, came out, and got their chickens. The Skid Row winos, shaky with the bars being closed for election, came out and got their bottles of muscatel. The elderly were marched wheezing out of their nursing homes, the low-income whites were watched by the precinct captains as they left for work in the morning and reminded that they had to stop at the polling place. That night, Daley sat in the Morrison with Lynch, Marovitz, and the party heavies, and an hour or two after the polls closed, the figures told him the story. It wasn't a landslide, but the 100,000-vote spread was decisive. The Machine had delivered as expected, but Kennelly's hoped for protest vote in the outlying neighborhoods had not materialized. He won nineteen wards, but by only a few thousand votes. Adamowski took three wards.

Kennelly accepted defeat like the nonprofessional he was, first threatening to throw his support to the Republican candidate, and finally deciding to do nothing, which surprised no one. After leaving office, he withdrew from public affairs, spending his time brooding, drinking, and calling his old aides in City Hall to tell them that Daley was doing a bad job. His sole pleasure was appearing on the same platform with Daley at civic luncheons and banquets and gloating because he got bigger ovations, while Daley flushed. But Daley had never put much store in banquets.

The Machine didn't slow as it turned toward the April 5 election. Naturally, that wouldn't have been anything to worry about. But instead of dragging out an obscure victim, the Republicans surprised everybody by finding a genuine candidate in Ald. Robert Merriam. Actually, he found them, since Merriam was a Democrat who had switched parties because he didn't like the company he was keeping. He had succeeded Senator Douglas as alderman of the Fifth Ward, the University of Chicago area and center of the intellectual and liberal establishment. Years earlier, his father, a political-science professor, had represented the ward and was known as the "conscience" of the City Council, no small job in the days of the aldermanic Gray Wolves. Young Merriam, carrying on the tradition, had pushed for liberal and progressive reforms. He didn't get many, though, because the aldermen of his day, while not as blatantly venal as in his father's time, were as ignorant and bigoted. A splendid orator, good-looking, knowledgeable, energetic, and youthfully mature, Merriam would have been expected to crush Daley in any city but Chicago. As it stood, he was an underdog, but a dangerous one. His campaign was adequately financed by the Republican business establishment, and he had a hustling staff and was developing volunteer ward organizations. He needed the volunteers because about half the Republican ward committeemen had been bought off with jobs or money by their Democratic counterparts or disliked Merriam for his liberal views.

Merriam stayed on the attack throughout the spring campaign, hammering at corruption in the Police Department, and the Machine. Daley's answer was, "Where is your proof, where is your evidence?" Luckily for Merriam, one of Daley's running mates provided some of the evidence. In mid-campaign, the Machine's candidate for city clerk was exposed as having acted as attorney in zoning cases he had voted on in the City Council.

The Chicago Bar Association moved against him, so Daley had to drop him from the ticket and find a replacement. He made a clever move, though, and actually strengthened the ticket. Morris B. Sachs, a popular department store owner, had run with Kennelly for city clerk. The night they lost, Sachs became part of one of the most famous news pictures in the city's history, wrapping his arms around the taller Kennelly's neck and resting his sobbing, contorted face on his chest. Daley called Sachs and asked him to join his team as the city clerk candidate. Sachs wrapped his arms around Daley's neck and beamed.

In a novel move, Merriam raised the issue of vote fraud before the election took place. Most candidates waited until fraud took place before complaining, which was too late. Merriam sent thousands of postcards to names taken from the lists of registered voters in Machine wards. Many came back stamped addressee unknown or deceased.

He also got help from an unusual character named Admiral Leroy, who, as a West Side precinct captain, was an expert in the filching of votes. Leroy had quit his ward organization to run against the regular candidate for alderman. He didn't run because some men came to his home and told him that if he did, he would be shot. Instead, he went to Merriam and volunteered to help him. During the primary, Admiral Leroy was sent by Merriam into a West Side polling place with a hidden wire recorder and a tiny camera. The polling place was in the precinct run by Short Pencil Louie, known as one of the outstanding vote thieves in the city, and Leroy came away with pictures of Short Pencil Louis erasing Kennelly's X's, and writing them in for Daley. It caused a fine flap and the Election Board had no choice but to conduct an inquiry. The result was that the Machine-controlled Election Board censured Merriam and Admiral Leroy. But Merriam's vote fraud hunt made headlines in at least three of the papers. Surprisingly, one paper, the Hearst's *American,* had switched their support to Daley and labeled Merriam a Democratic turncoat. The *American* decided that Daley was a man of vision and potential greatness. It was also rumored that Daley had promised the editor that his precinct captains would push subscriptions for the paper, which at the time had the lowest circulation in the city.

Meanwhile, Daley was taking the high road in his campaign, trying to ignore Merriam's attacks while presenting himself as a hard-working, dedicated, churchgoing family man, and most of all, a neighborhood guy. His favorite phrase was: "When I walk down the streets of my neighborhood, I see the streets of every neighborhood. When I go to my church, I see the churches of every faith. When I greet my children, I see the children of every faith." He portrayed himself as the candidate of the little neighborhood people, fighting, protecting their interests against the big men of State Street. "The sun will rise over all the Chicago neighborhoods," he told the street-corner rallies, "instead of just State Street." As they cheered, they had no way of knowing that the downtown interests would prosper most under his administration, and the neighborhoods least. As he had always done, Daley refused to attack his opponent directly. "Let's talk about the issues. I do not believe in dealing in personalities." Privately, he complained bitterly to friends about the charge that he would open up the town, and told them that one of his daughters had come to him and said, "Daddy, is it true that if you are mayor there will be open gambling and prostitution?" Nevertheless, while Daley avoided attacking his opponent, the Machine was traveling its usual course.

Merriam had been divorced from his college sweetheart, the marriage a wartime casualty. The Machine's agents sent out unsigned letters saying nobody knew how many children he had abandoned without support. Copies of his divorce papers were circulated in Catholic neighborhoods. Alderman Keane, an instinctive gut fighter, went on television and made snide remarks about the divorce. Then a rumor was spread in white neighborhoods that Merriam's second wife, who was born in France, was part Negro. Even before the phrase "white backlash" was coined, the Machine knew how to use it. Letters from a nonexistent "American Negro Civic Association" were sent into outlying residential areas, urging a vote for Merriam because he would see to it that Negroes found homes and building sites in all parts of the city. Another phony letter from a "Taft-Eisenhower League" asked voters to reject him because he hung around with left-wingers. Somebody even put letters under windshield wipers in congested neighborhoods urging a vote for Merriam because he supported a ban on overnight street parking.

It was a vicious campaign, and as party chairman, Daley

could not have been unaware of some of the tactics. But just as he held himself above the Mafia while tolerating its existence in his organization, and just as he did not share in the Springfield graft while working with those who did, he did not personally join in the mudslinging. His virtue remained as intact as his hypocrisy.

Despite the Machine, there were times during the campaign when reporters believed that Merriam was ahead. The vote fraud charges had aroused people. If the election had been held ten days earlier than it was, some reporters believe, Merriam would have won. But on April 5 Daley received 708,222 votes to Merriam's 589,555. The Machine functioned well. Merriam won nineteen wards, a strong showing, but in most of them his vote percentage was about fifty-two to fifty-eight percent. Only in the strong Republican wards did he get as much as sixty-five percent. It wasn't enough to counter the awesome power shown in the Machine wards, notably in Dawson's black precincts. Dawson brought his three wards in fifty-seven thousand to sixteen thousand. And the famous Twenty-fourth Ward on the West Side delivered itself 18,300 to 1,500.

By mid-evening, the screaming, sweating crowd couldn't move or hear itself in the lobby, corridors, and outer offices of the Morrison Hotel headquarters. Police pushed through a path for the labor leaders, the ward bosses, and the political judges who were admitted to the inner room. Finally, Daley came out to make his victory statement and to pose for pictures. His administration began at that instant, in the memory of a ward leader:

"When the photographers were let in for the pictures, Daley stiff-armed Arvey, Horan, and Gill right out of them. You never saw such stiff arms, and you could see the one-man rule starting right there and then. Jesus, was Horan mad. He didn't talk to Daley for a year and a half. Arvey was through that night, too, only he was too smart to let on. Daley pushed him right out of the party, but he let Arvey stay as national committeeman, because it didn't mean anything, and sit on the park board, because that didn't mean anything either. That way people in other parts of the country would think that Arvey was still big heat here, and when they were going to do business in Chicago, they'd go to his law firm because they

wanted somebody who could pull strings. But since
Daley came in, Arvey hasn't had any more weight in the
organization than a good precinct captain. Daley didn't
want any of those guys identified with him. Once he took
over, he put them down."

Daley's rebuff should have settled the still unanswered
question of whether he would remain as party chairman.
Before the election, some of the party leaders had suggested to him that it might be a good idea for him to resign
and rid himself of the "boss" stigma. Daley listened but
wouldn't commit himself. He said he'd make up his mind
after the election. And after the election he decided to retain the chairmanship. He has since given several different
versions of how he reached the decision. Sometimes he
says, "I tendered my resignation as chairman, but they
refused to accept it." Technically, this is correct, but if
anybody had reached out to accept it, his hand would
have been chopped off. To the gullible Daley offers this
version: after the election, he set up a blackboard in the
basement of his home, and he and Sis spent the evening
chalking in the pluses and minuses of retaining both posts;
they found that the pluses exceeded the minuses, and
together they agreed that for the good of the city he should
hold all the power. Picture that: a man who spent most
of his adult life in politics and government, a man so professional that he was able to rise to the top of the most
competitive municipal political organization in the country, having to jot on a blackboard what it all means.

Most likely, the answer is made up of several elements.
First, he believed that he was better at either job than
anybody else in the party. He knew the Machine from the
bottom to the top, having been at both extremes and at
every level between. The same could be said for his credentials to be mayor. Like the comptroller of a corporation, he had spent his years in government always near
the financing, the budget, the spending, and the income,
while others were making speeches. Second, he does not
view the party and the city as being creatures apart. They
are one: the Democratic party is the city, and Republicans and independents are simply misguided people who
don't understand how things work. The party is the political voice of the city, and the city government is the ma-

chinery to activate their wishes. Thus his slogan: "Good government is good politics." Finally, if someone else became chairman, the sonofabitch might do to him what he did to Kennelly. By remaining chairman, he would decide who ran for office, every office, permitting him to control the rise of any potential competition. It's no accident that in his fifteen years as chairman and mayor, not a single young political figure would rise through the party to a position of being his obvious successor. Good sturdy mediocrities would be the rule. He would not share power because it is difficult to share. Pat Nash, when he was chairman, had overruled Mayor Kelly. This wouldn't happen to Daley. The adage was: "You run the party or it runs you." That was all he had to write on his blackboard.

On the evening of April 20, 1955, three thousand party leaders and their families squeezed into the City Council chambers, and Daley, with his family at his side, took the oath of office from Judge Marovitz, ending the tradition of the outgoing mayor swearing in his successor.

The very next morning, the man who plodded for so long, moving step by step, inch by inch, took off at a gallop. He had four years to make liars of his opponents, believers of the suspicious, and he wasn't going to waste a minute. They would be four of the busiest, most frantic years City Hall had ever seen without people being indicted.

Money was the first project. The fastest way to show people that something is happening is to build things. The money had to be found at home, because with Eisenhower in Washington, the days of the big federal grants had not yet come. And raising it at home meant doing business with the legislature and its rustics who, because of the outdated state constitution, decided how distant cities could tax themselves. Kennelly had always been afraid to ask the legislature for new taxing powers, but Daley headed for Springfield.

As always, the legislature in 1955 was dominated by downstate Republicans. Even worse, when Stevenson vacated the governor's mansion to run for president in 1952, he was succeeded by a Republican, William Stratton.

Stratton, however, was a practical politician and som

one Daley could do business with. By the end of the legislative session that summer, Daley had an increase in the sales tax and a new utility tax. He had the money to get started. Why was Stratton so cooperative? Why would he help a Democrat make himself look good? Some say it was Daley's skills of persuasion, his knowledge of legislative give and take, all of which are not inconsiderable. Others said Stratton simply agreed that Chicago needed the things Daley wanted. Others, especially politicians, say Daley promised Stratton that he would run a patsy against him in 1956. Daley turned purple and pounded his fist on the lecterns when he later denied the rumor. But he did indeed run a patsy against Stratton in 1956.

With the money coming in, the next step was to make sure that he, not the aldermen, did the spending. He quickly moved to strip them of the powers they had enjoyed during Kennelly's days. The council had always made the city's budget. That ended. Daley would create the budget, then almost half a billion a year. It was the first and biggest step in changing the council from a legislative body to a rubber stamp for his administration. Few of the aldermen protested. It meant less work, thus freeing them for other activities, such as the pursuit of personal wealth. They squawked, however, but then submitted, when he took away what appeared to be a petty power, the granting of driveway permits. This was a steady source of graft, with each alderman controlling the permits in his ward.

Builders of apartment houses, restaurants, gas stations, and anyone else who needed a driveway, included in their planned costs the "drop" to the alderman. Daley removed the power because it was a potential source of embarrassment and trouble. The aldermen could learn to use a little imagination and finesse.

The first year was splashy, as he intended it to be. With no major elections until late 1956, he could concentrate on generating an atmosphere of movement and accomplishment in City Hall. He concentrated first on goals that ᵈld bring quick, visible results: hiring more policemen ˜men, putting double construction shifts on the ˜ressway, street lighting, paving. Hardly a day ⁺he announcement of a new project being started or planned. Surprisingly, the axe did not fall on the Kennelly cabinet members. Since they were Democrats anyway, it wasn't essential that they be fired. By retaining them, he didn't have to delay his fast start. And there is nobody as loyal as the man who shuffles in expecting to be fired and bounces out with a pat on the back and a reprieve. Daley went even further, giving them raises. He made only one change, firing the fire commissioner and putting in his old Hamburg Club buddy, Robert Quinn.

There was time, too, for political revenge. Daley has always been portrayed by his apologists as a man who "does not keep books." He lets bygones be bygones, they say, and is always happy to welcome back the wayward.

To the contrary, he does not forget even a petty slight, and will wait years, if he has to, to get revenge. His skill is in doing it quietly, but that wasn't possible in his first official act of revenge after being elected. Frank Keenan, who had defied him by managing Kennelly's campaign, had to be punished. The only way Keenan could have avoided it was by coming to Daley, admitting his sins, and asking forgiveness. This, after all, is what Daley did every Saturday in the confessional booth of his church, making his apologies to a higher authority. He waited for Keenan to do the same. But Keenan, always a rebellious type, didn't kneel. Daley set out to break him. First he tried to oust Keenan as ward committeeman by running someone against him in the election for ward leadership. Keenan survived the challenge, which enraged Daley even further. It would have been better for Keenan if he had lost, because the state's attorney, a Democrat, then brought criminal charges against him for illegally exempting property from the tax rolls. Anybody who has ever been assessor could have been indicted for the same thing, and probably a dozen other infractions, because giving tax breaks is the reason the assessor's office is so politically important. For a Democratic state's attorney to go after a Democratic officeholder was unheard of, which is why retaining the prosecutor's office was a "must." Keenan replied that the indictments were ordered by Daley, and he was later acquitted. But his troubles had begun. He soon became a Republican, and he finally spent time in prison for income tax evasion. Some, or all, of his troubles could have been avoided if he had gone to confession in City Hall.

The second act of vengeance was executed smoothly and quietly, the way Daley prefers. During the primary, a police captain who had headed the department's special Syndicate investigation unit, and a dedicated Kennelly man, had tapped the phones at the Morrison Hotel headquarters; but Daley learned of the tap. After the election, the special unit was disbanded and the policeman, the nation's leading expert in Syndicate affairs, was permanently assigned to trying to solve murders that had occurred years earlier. His second in command, another Syndicate expert, was assigned to a station in the quietest residential neighborhood in the city.

Such sport aside, Daley was having a joyous first term. The Democratic National Convention came to Chicago, putting Daley in the national limelight for the first time as leader of the Illinois delegates, most of whom he selected. He helped nominate Stevenson for a second opportunity to be beaten by Eisenhower, although many of the Illinois delegates weren't for Stevenson. But Daley owed Stevenson for his support during the mayoralty election.

The newspapers were doing their third 360-degree turn on what kind of man Daley was. In 1946, when he ran for sheriff, he had been a tool of Kelly. When he joined Stevenson's cabinet, he became part of a new breed of clean politician. When he dumped Kennelly, he became a political boss. But when he started spending funds in the direction of improving the downtown business district, he became an inspiring city leader. The civic leaders and businessmen who had rushed to Kennelly's defense were now joining in the praise for Daley. Kennelly had never done any of the things for them that Daley was doing. He put big bond issue referendums on the ballot to raise funds for the start of public works projects. The banks were delighted at the prospect of bidding on the profitable bonds. He announced that high-rise apartments were the administration's official answer to the suburban exodus, and that the lake front and the central city would someday bristle with the residential skyscrapers. The banks and real estate interests were enthralled. Planned expressways, all of them leading to the downtown business section, would be put on a crash, priority, hurry-up, round-the-clock schedule, and more parking garages would be built to accommodate the motorized shoppers, and the downtown stores were ecstatic. O'Hare Airport, then used only by the air force, would be rushed along to meet the jet age, bringing more and more convention business to the city. And a convention hall would be built on Chicago's lake front, despite the protests of conservationists. "Boss" Daley was suddenly "Dick the Builder," the man who was getting things going, revitalizing the city, pumping new life into the old town.

With everybody cheering, his bond issue went through easily, and work was beginning. The biggest expenditures were for O'Hare Airport, bridges and train crossings, street lights and lake docking facilities, new police stations, and sewers. Out of $113 million in bond revenue, only $20 million was to be used for slum land clearance and community conservation. But since the civic leaders, downtown merchants, and newspaper editors did not live in slums, it was not the sort of inequity that would bother them. Not that the slums, among the worst in the nation, did not interest them. In a one-month period, thirteen black adults and children died in a series of slum fires. Most of the buildings had been illegally converted to cubbyhole units. The newspapers' solution was to rake a few of the slum owners across the coals of public opinion. The fact that the city's building department was taking bribes faster than it could spend them was of less concern to them. The blacks were jammed into the ghettos because the city made no effort to crack the closed real estate market and let them out. During his gala first term, Daley allowed this policy to continue. His urban renewal program amounted to a stack full of charts and blueprints. Rats gnawed on black infants' feet, while money was used to build new police stations around the corner. The Daley years were underway with the values that would never change: things, concrete, glass, steel, downtown, business profit. Then if there's anything left, maybe something for the human being.

When he wasn't being praised for his projects, he was lauded for not having opened up the town after all. The

warnings of Kennelly and Merriam that the whoopee
days of Kelly-Nash would return had not materialized.
Everybody downtown agreed that, if anything, Chicago
had become even more sedate. The wire rooms, that in the
old days were as common as neighborhood drugstores, had
not reappeared. Whorehouses had not appeared. No, indeed, Chicago was not returning to those thrilling days of
yesteryear, and it was all thanks to the dynamic new
mayor.

But in the black belt, the Syndicate's drug business was
booming. Blacks, however, were expected to stick needles
in their arms. That was Bill Dawson's territory, anyway,
and there was nothing that could be done about the way
those people acted. And while it was true that one
couldn't walk into a wire room in any neighborhood, most
bartenders, newsstand operators, and corner cigar stores
would take your bet. The Syndicate's betting take was as
great as ever. Every downtown office building had its
bookie, and to this day there isn't a newspaper printing department, circulation dock, or mailing room that doesn't
have a bookie. The old-fashioned bordellos hadn't returned, but in a bar a block from City Hall, the dozen or
so twenty-five-dollar whores were waiting for somebody to
take them to the small hotel next door that handled almost
no other guests. Bars of the same kind operated across the
downtown area. In the Syndicate-run strip joints about
three blocks from police headquarters, the dancers busied
themselves between numbers, performing fellatio in the
booths for ten dollars a spasm. It wasn't necessary to
open up the town, because the town hadn't been shut
down. Kennelly's idea of reform was to put it behind the
curtains. Daley kept it there. The profits and the services
were the same.

If it hadn't been for the 1956 elections, Daley's first
term would have been perfection. It was a Republican
year, with Eisenhower rolling over Stevenson and Governor Stratton beating Daley's handpicked patsy. In fact,
the original patsy dropped out because of a scandal and
was replaced by an even softer patsy. The real political
jolt was at home in Cook County, where Ben Adamowski,
the frustrated Pole, switched parties and was elected, with
heavy suburban support, as state's attorney. Daley knew

Adamowski's plan. He had four years to get something on Daley, either directly or through other Machine creatures. As the county's chief prosecutor, he could haul Democrats before grand juries, obtain indictments, maybe send somebody to jail and, at the least, create a whirlwind of damaging publicity. Even if a flimsy case fell apart in court, the headlines could wreck a politician. Daley was aware of that. Look what his state's attorney had done to Frank Keenan.

Daley, however, had time on his side.

Adamowski took office in January 1957. It takes months to recruit a new staff of investigators. The state's attorney's one-hundred-man investigative unit is made up, for the most part, of politically influential policemen on loan from the Chicago department. First, Adamowski would have to find policemen he could trust, then he would have to get them transferred. Daley's police commissioner, still in City Hall, could deny or delay the transfers. It also takes time to replace the assistant state's attorneys with lawyers who were Republicans. And they would have to be willing to work for minimal salaries, because the Machine controlled the County Board, which set budgets for all county offices, and it wasn't throwing any extra money Adamowski's way. As eager as Adamowski was to pursue Daley and other Democrats, he could not forget that he had to build a respectable prosecution record with the day-to-day criminal cases that would occupy most of his staff's time. Adamowski's political hunt would take place, Daley knew, but it wouldn't begin for a long time, and when it did begin, it would take time for him to find something. And by then, Daley's first term would probably be over.

Meanwhile, nothing Adamowski did could reverse the change that was occurring in the city's political alignment. The big Republicans, men who had money and influence with the papers, were seeing the new Daley, the Daley who understood their needs, and they liked what they saw. His vision of the city was the same as theirs: downtown first. Revitalize the Loop and the nearby commercial areas and the rest of the city would follow.

Even the eastern magazines took notice. They read about his achievements in the Chicago press and did stories of their own. Then the Chicago papers printed stories about the magazine stories, as confirmation of their earlier stories. The propaganda was being poured as thickly as the overpriced highway concrete. Little was said about the passing of four years with almost nothing being done about the growing deterioration of the neighborhoods. An old Bridgeport pal with no qualifications had been put in charge of the community conservation program. Edwin Berry, new director of the local branch of the Urban League, came in from out of town and was given a fast handshake and faster brush-off by City Hall. He was appalled by the ghettos, and when he said Chicago was the most residentially segregated city in the country, the *Tribune* called him a liar. The schools had not improved, although new school buildings were planned. Always, a structure was the answer. So more and more families moved to the suburbs, with better schools their prime objective. The last of the city's vacant land, all across the outer neighborhoods, was being snapped up by developers while City Hall waived its last opportunity to use the land to decentralize the public housing projects by scattering smaller, livable projects throughout the city. In effect, it officially condoned segregation.

The Syndicate was still putting bodies in sewers and in car trunks, bombing its way into control of the restaurant industry's supply and union needs, and had murdered its way into a take-over of the black policy wheels. Public transportation service was declining, with all the emphasis on expressways. One of the worst city public health departments in the country, politically corrupt, was no better after four years. City inspectors of all kinds were shaking citizens down, as were the police. And in traffic court an entire department did nothing but fix tickets. But downtown was happy, so there was no way Daley could be stopped in 1959, and the Republican city politicians knew it.

One of them was Timothy Sheehan, a fish importer, who had been a congressman from the far Northwest Side, a Republican area. Sheehan will never forget 1959.

"I had been on vacation while the Republican Central Committee was looking for a candidate. They brought in several well-known businessmen and tried to talk them into running, but none of them wanted to. They asked me to run, but I didn't want to. But they insisted, so I told them that if they'd promise to let me run against Senator Douglas in 1960, I'd go for mayor in 1959. They agreed. Of course they broke their promise later, but I didn't know that. So I ran for mayor. I wasn't surprised when all the Republican businessmen started coming out for Daley. It was a practical decision on their part. They figure if you can't beat 'em, join 'em. And most of them are under obligations. They were all getting favors from City Hall. I went around to all the papers and asked for their endorsement, but I was just going through the motions, and I knew I didn't have a chance. The *Tribune* said the most they would do is suggest that the Republicans vote for the Republicans, and the Democrats for the Democrats. Another problem I had was that there hadn't been any really big scandals during his first term. All you can do in that kind of situation is to try and not let yourself be disgraced. That's what I did. I didn't say anything stupid, like predicting that I'd win."

Nobody else predicted it either. Daley hardly campaigned, limiting himself to appearances before prestigious civic groups and pep-talk meetings at ward organizations. He could sit back and watch with satisfaction as the biggest business and civic leaders in Chicago, who only four years earlier had been fighting him, all added their good names to the newly created Nonpartisan Committee for the Reelection of Mayor Daley. The committee included people like the president of an airline that would soon be landing its planes at the big, new O'Hare Airport; the State Street merchants, delighted by the new parking garages going up on the ruins of architectural landmarks; the president of the University of Chicago, which would soon begin uprooting blacks as urban renewal reshaped the land around the campus to the image and value of its choice. The hundreds of prominent names on the new committee had two things in common: they or their companies or institutions stood to profit from Daley's policies, and most of them lived out in an expensive suburb.

Sheehan campaigned, but with so little attention paid to him by the press, a street-corner survey might have shown that most Chicagoans couldn't identify him.

Daley's campaign statements, handed to reporters by his press aide, were a recitation of his accomplishments: new street lights, new mechanical street sweepers, new bridges and overpasses, paving, resurfacing, new police stations. He didn't have to tell the people downtown what their gifts were.

The Machine rolled, and the only person happier than Daley to see election day come and go was Sheehan, the reluctant victim. Daley got 71.4 percent of the vote, and won by a majority of 466,672.

The West Side's Twenty-fourth Ward, the poorest, most slum-plagued black area in the city, still dominated by white precinct captains, turned out a vote of 20,300 to 800. Sheehan said he was surprised that he got the eight hundred. Daley won forty-nine wards, and Sheehan one—his own.

Elated, Daley and Sis hopped a plane for a vacation in the Florida Keys. He could relax and reflect on the four-year miracle he had preformed. The bad guy had become the good guy, the almost great guy. The Republican party in the city, after its 1955 revival, was again entombed, its money men now sending their checks to the Morrison. He had whipped his Machine into line, shelved the old competitors, purged the incorrigibles. Adamowski was still looking, but so far he wasn't finding.

And with the Eisenhower years ending, there could be a Machine governor in his future, maybe a friendly Democrat in the White House. He had done it. Everything had gone according to plan. Even the tarpon were biting, and he dragged out a seventy-pounder. That would give him something to tell the friendly City Hall press room about when he got back.

If he had known what was simmering, waiting to explode after he got back, he might have jumped overboard and joined the tarpons.

Chapter VI

KUNSTLER: Now, Mayor Daley, how many executive departments do you have in the City of Chicago?

WITNESS: Approximately 35.

KUNSTLER: Have you ever had occasion to remove the head of any executive department?

FORAN: Objection, your Honor.

HOFFMAN: I sustain the objection.

KUNSTLER: Have you ever had occasion to remove the superintendent of police?

FORAN: Objection.

HOFFMAN: I sustain the objection.

The desk sergeant was drunk. Not so drunk that he couldn't ramble about the good old days, when he peeled down to the waist and fought the toughest mug in the district toe to toe in the back room of the station, but drunk enough so that he lolled in a chair and let a young patrolman handle the phone calls and the people who came in off the street with problems. The sergeant got drunk early every evening. But by midnight, when his shift ended, he'd be coming out of it enough to drive the fifteen miles to his home on the far South Side.

He'd complain about the long drive every night, and

always working the night trick, but when somebody asked him why he didn't get transferred to a district near his home and rotate his shift, he'd say, "I got expenses. My wife's health isn't good. And it took me years to get some of these taverns lined up. I can't leave that now."

It was a practical explanation. Some taverns paid him to stay open beyond the 2 A.M. closing hour. He was less expensive than a 4 A.M. license. Others paid him to assure that if a bartender worked a customer over, the customer would be charged with assault. He didn't keep it all: the detectives on his shift got some, and the lieutenant in a little office in the back got more. And his collection was small change compared to what the captain's bag man picked up during the day.

The captain's bag man made the rounds of the bookies, the homosexual bars, the hotels and lounges that were headquarters for prostitution rings. That's where the real money was, but the captain didn't keep it all. He got some, but most of it went to the ward committeeman. That's why the captain was running the station: the ward committeeman had put him there because he trusted him to collect the payoffs and give an honest accounting and a fair split. If he didn't, the ward committeeman would call downtown to headquarters and have the captain transferred to a paper-shuffling job somewhere. Not that this was likely to happen: the captain knew what he was supposed to do, or the ward boss wouldn't have had him promoted through the ranks all the way to captain.

While the sergeant on the near North Side was nipping from his bottle and waiting for midnight, the sergeant at a South Side police station was ducking out the side door to get a beer in the tavern right across the street from the station. A hulking lesbian drew a glass for him, and at a table in the back one of a half-dozen black girls waved and said, "Hi, Sergeant." He laughed and winked. While he sipped his beer, a man came in, went to the back, talked to the big lesbian, then went out through the back door with one of the girls. Stairs led to rooms upstairs. He'd pay the girl twenty dollars, out of which the girl would keep about half. The lesbian would get the other half, and out of that she would eventually pay the captain's bag man a certain amount, and he would give it to the captain, and the captain would give some to the ward committeeman, and spread the rest down the ranks to the sergeant and others. The girls were a real force in the economy.

When the sergeant finished his beer, he returned to the station and got back behind the desk. Two vice detectives came out of the back and yelled to him, "We're gonna root around, Sarge," which meant they were going to look for a few drifting hookers, pimps, or junkies and shake them down. Not everybody was lined up by the captain's bag man.

A black man walked into the station and stood by the desk, mumbling and holding his hands over his stomach, which was bleeding. He had been in a fight and somebody cut him. The sergeant looked disgusted. He handed the man a newspaper. The man looked confused and held the newspaper as if to read it. "No, dummy," the sergeant said, "go on over there by the wall and stand on it." He didn't want the man bleeding near the desk. The man did as he was told, the blood dripping on the paper. The sergeant told the patrolman to call downtown to the radio room. "See if you can get the wagon to take this guy to the county." About an hour and a couple of pints of blood later, the paddy wagon came and took the man to the county hospital. There were at least two private hospitals closer, but they did not welcome blacks in their emergency room.

Meanwhile, on the Outer Drive, two policemen in a squad car spotted a speeder. They flipped on their red light and one of them played the spotlight on the car's rear window. The motorist pulled onto the shoulder, stopped, took out his license, folded a ten-dollar bill around it, and handed it to one of the policemen. The policeman put the ten dollars in his pocket, cautioned the man against speeding, returned the license, and they parted. The motorist was the kind the policeman liked. If he had been shy, or dense, the policeman would have had to stand there, hemming and hawing, trying to get the message across. That failing, he would have signed and written a ticket. There's no profit in tickets, but fortunately most Chicagoans weren't shy or dense.

On the Southwest Side, another policeman stopped a

motorist and used a different approach when the motorist didn't gift wrap his license. He carried wooden pencils in his pocket, and he would announce: "I have three kinds of pencils which I sell—a five-dollar pencil, a ten-dollar pencil, and a twenty-five-dollar pencil. I think you need a ten-dollar pencil, don't you?" The pencils were seldom sold for more than twenty-five dollars, because that would have meant somebody had been run over, and fixing that required the cooperation of prosecutors and even judges and was not something that could be arranged on the scene.

While the policeman was selling pencils, a police captain in a $200 suit and $25 shoes, purchased on a salary of $180 a week, was telling some friends in an expensive restaurant about the suspected burglar a couple of his men brought in. The suspect had been working a street of wealthy apartment-house dwellers. Burglaries in such apartments brought publicity and complaints from influential people, problems police captains tried to avoid. "They brought him into my office and I took out my .38 special and pointed it right between his eyes and cocked it. He opened his mouth to yell and I shoved it in, right to his tonsils, and I told him, 'You sonofabitch, I don't want you stealing in my district. You want to steal, you go steal in somebody else's district, but if I catch you here again, I'll blow your fucking head off!' " There was nothing more the captain could do, since the man hadn't been caught stealing.

Somewhere else, a suspected thief was shoved into a room in the back of a station. The detectives followed him in, put him in a chair, and while two of them held his arms, a third picked up a phone book. Unlike a rubber hose or a wooden club, a phone book does not leave bruises, but after being hit on the head often enough a man feels like his spine has been compressed into a one-inch cube. The suspect would confess to almost every unsolved theft on the station's books, providing a fine clean-up record for the detectives.

In a hospital emergency room, a man awoke on a table. When they brought him in, he was covered with blood and looked close to death. He had run his car into a light pole. As it turned out, he wasn't seriously hurt, just cut

rested, a few places closed down, and a few weeks later it would return to normal.

The condition of the Police Department was no secret to anyone, including the newspapers. They all had police reporters, but they viewed their jobs as getting stories about crimes, which required the friendship of policemen. It was not uncommon for reporters to turn in a story about a man confessing to a crime without the fact that he had been pummeled a bit by the detectives before making the confession.

Most Chicagoans considered the dishonesty of the police as part of the natural environment. The Chicago River is polluted, the factories belch smoke, the Cubs are the North Side team, the Sox are the South Side team, George Halas owns the Bears, and the cops are crooked—so what else was new?

In many ways, the citizens preferred a dishonest Police Department. The traffic bribe saved a trip to court. The tavern payoff was in return for favors granted. And if you wore a suit, a tie, and were clean shaven, the cop had to be careful about how he treated you, because he didn't know but what you were a friend of an alderman, in which case you could take his billy club and beat him without a whimper.

That's the way the Police Department was in 1955, when Daley became mayor, and it was the same, and maybe worse, in 1960. He knew about it because it would have been impossible not to. He grew up in politics and the police force was part of the Machine. But nobody was complaining, at least nobody of importance. When *Life* magazine wrote in 1957 that Chicago's police were the most corrupt in the nation, Daley raged about the "unwarranted slur" and defended his police as being among the finest in the nation. They were among the finest only in the cut of their civilian attire and in their choice of cars and diamond pinky rings. Even if Daley had wanted to reform them, and there was no indication that the idea crossed his mind, it would have been an unpleasant job. Some policemen worked as precinct captains. Others were assigned to watch polling places on election days, to assure that there would be no interference with the acts of fraud. They were a source of income and influence for his ward bosses. To tamper with the Police Department would have been politically unwise. And in January 1960, he had enough problems without looking for others.

The euphoria of his first term and landslide reelection had dissolved in 1959 with not one, but two, major scandals in his administration. Adamowski dug into the traffic courts system and came up with the not unsurprising fact that its main function seemed to be the fixing of tickets. Some court employees did nothing else. If it hadn't been for the hapless black motorist, nobody would have been paying fines. And in the middle of the mess was Daley's old friend, Joe Gill, who was, at the time, in charge of the municipal court employees. The fact that tickets were being fixed didn't surprise anybody, but the extent of the practice did. Mainly, the scandal served as a reminder to the city that for all the hoopla about public works projects and dynamic leadership, the Machine still thrived on the fundamental fix.

The other scandal was more interesting because it was something new, and that in itself was unusual. In Chicago, most scandals repeat themselves. If a government agency gets in trouble and a reform is instituted, a few years later they will be back in business again.

In the second scandal, bail bondsmen were getting their money back from the courts after their customers jumped bail. This obviously defeated the purpose of bail, which is to assure that the defendant will appear in court. The money was being ordered returned by the chief justice of the municipal court to bondsmen who included his social friends, people who gave him gifts, and Mafia types. The bail bond business had always attracted people who should have been in cells themselves. They made their living hanging around police stations, paying policemen to alert them to prospective customers. A desk sergeant, after booking somebody for a crime, would ask him if he could make bond. If not, the sergeant would call his favorite bondsman, who would post bond, pay off the sergeant, and charge the accused interest when the case was over. If the accused didn't show up, the bondsman would hunt him down faster than the police did to protect his investment. But the chief justice saved them the effort by ordering that the bond forfeitures be vacated.

These were quiet times in the nation and the world, so the papers could print page after page of scandal news, day after day, and Adamowski made sure that there was something to print. On days when he wasn't bringing new witnesses before a grand jury, he'd say that he was planning to bring new witnesses. Then after they testified, he'd announce that even new sensational sins had been discovered. One thing always leads to another in a scandal, and these two seemed to go on forever, at least for Daley.

His approach was to look innocent and say that his office had nothing at all to do with such things, since Gill was an elected official, and so was the chief justice of the municipal court. The scandals were theirs, not his. But since everybody took orders from him, nobody was impressed by his pose, and behind the scenes he was trying to find a way out. This is when his public relations program began.

To counter the scandal news, Daley tried to make Chicago a "fun city." He hoped that by staging circus-like events he could drive the scandals off the front page, if not out of the grand jury. Queen Elizabeth was invited to visit Chicago during an American tour and City Hall inflated the event into something approaching a world's fair. Proper perspective was provided, however, by Ald. Paddy Bauler, an old rogue who boycotted the Queen's banquet and spent the evening in his tavern, watching the event on television and shouting "fuck you" to reporters who asked him why he hadn't attended. The Pan-American games, a track meet, was brought to Chicago, a city that has little enthusiasm for track events, and it was boomed as the greatest thing since the first olympics. Something called "Venetian Night" was inaugurated, an evening when boat owners paraded their yachts along the lake front. Daley was so anxious for a big crowd that he called in a prominent businessman, who was head of a nonpolitical citizen's committee that worked on problems of the aged, and asked him to round up the old people in the nursing homes and the city's public housing for the elderly and bring them down to the lake front.

"I told him that I couldn't do that," the businessman said. "You can't just haul old people around the city by the thousands and make them sit out on the lake front in the night air, and without sanitation facilities nearby. But he insisted that they would enjoy it. When I told him that I wouldn't do it, he became exasperated and threw up his hands and said: 'Why do I have so much trouble with you in doing things for the citizens of this city?' "

Even a pennant won by the Chicago White Sox was grabbed by City Hall as a great civic event—but with disastrous results. The night the Sox clinched it, Daley's fire chief, Robert Quinn, turned on the city's entire civil defense siren system to celebrate the championship. However, he had not warned anybody that he was going to do it, so most of the city's 3,700,000 citizens thought the wailing of sirens at 11 P.M. meant they were about o go up in a nuclear cloud. Thousands of them poured into the streets, called the police and newspapers, prayed, wept, and became hysterical. Quinn's resignation was justifiably demanded by outraged citizens, but he is Daley's old Hamburg Club pal and was forgiven that and many future acts of inspired stupidity. He would someday attempt to prove his firemen's fitness by sending them on a ten-mile jog down the center of the Kennedy Expressway at the peak of rush hour, causing one monumental traffic jam.

As frantically as he tried to hide the scandals behind the fun-city smokescreen, there was no way Daley could avoid the reality of precinct captains under indictment, his chief justice in deep trouble, and the endless headlines about "Adamowski widens probe." No question about it, 1959, which had begun so gloriously, had turned into a bad year. It dramatized the challenge of trying to pose as a progressive leader while maintaining a profiteering, corrupt political organization. But if 1959 had been a bad year, it was just a prelude to the miseries of 1960.

In early January, while Daley and his wife were vacationing in the Florida Keys, he got a call from one of his aides preparing him for potential disaster. The word was that a professional thief had been arrested and, to save his own neck, had told the public defender about the unique membership of his burglary gang: the other members were Chicago cops. The information had reached Adamowski and, if it were true, there was no way a scandal could be averted. Because of their foolish effort to cover it up, the Chicago police had missed the chance to at least make their own arrests and show a willingness to clean house. Ald. Tom Keane later said, "Word had been going around for about two weeks before it came out, but the guys in the commissioner's office spent all their time trying to prove that it hadn't happened. Then Adamowski got wind of it and seized on it."

By the time Daley got back to Chicago, the headlines were as big and black as he had ever seen them. The policemen had been arrested by Adamowski's office, stolen merchandise recovered in their homes. They had been carrying the loot away in squad cars while on duty, and they had been at it for two years or more. At least eight policemen had been involved, including the son of a captain and several veterans on the force. It was immediately dubbed the "Summerdale Scandal," the policemen were called "the Burglars in Blue," and Adamowski's prize witness, a young thief named Richard Morrison, was labeled "the Babbling Burglar" because of his willingness to talk about everybody and everything.

Everybody in the Summerdale station was under suspicion, and the scandal was spreading faster than the plague. By the second day the details were pouring out of Adamowski's office and there was talk that it would involve dozens, hundreds, of policemen in other districts.

The public was genuinely shocked. It's one thing to take a few bucks to overlook an illegal u-turn; but even Chicagoans could become indignant at the thought of policemen jimmying the locks of appliance stores and loading up their trunks, on city time yet.

Daley went into a walking stupor, caused partly by shock and fear and partly by an increase in his usually modest Scotch intake. One of his committeemen recalls: "He really started putting it away, every night. For a couple of weeks there he was in terrible shape. There were days when it was all Sis could do to get him to leave the house in the morning, he was that afraid to face the thing. After that first term, with everything going so great, it was all caving in on him."

Haggard, his eyes red, Daley held press conferences and, in pleading tone, vowed that the Police Department would be cleaned up, reformed. There were no more angry denials that his Police Department was corrupt, no more demands for proof from the critics. The proof was out in the open. If they were working as burglars when they were supposed to be catching them, it was safe to assume that everything else that had been said about the Police Department was true.

After the initial shock, Daley felt cornered and harassed, and it soon showed in his reaction to questioning. When reporters asked him what he was doing about the police, he would stare at them coldly and say, "Next question." One morning he began screaming about corruption being part of the human condition, that it was found in all walks of life, all professions. "There are even crooked reporters," he shouted, "and I can spit on some from right here." When they demanded that he name them, he sagged and said, "I withdraw that statement."

"He was distraught," said Alderman Seymour Simon, then one of the rising stars of Daley's organization. "He was run-down and in bad shape physically, exhausted. Daley knew about the ordinary graft, but it genuinely shocked him that his cops were going out and working as burglars. Daley always figured that there would always be the ordinary kind of graft, and when it came to graft, he figures live and let live. But if you're caught you're on your own."

In this one, Daley was on his own. He was being blamed for the scandal, and it was an uncomfortable feeling. He had to shift the blame, find a sacrificial victim. The choice was obvious. As someone later wrote about the police chief, Timothy O'Connor: "O'Connor awoke that morning, looked in the mirror, and saw a goat."

O'Connor was generally acknowledged to be a good cop, honest and hard-working. He had made a reputation in the robbery detail, one of the few units where graft wasn't a way of life, since it is not wise to negotiate with an armed stickup man. He had been appointed police chief by Kennelly, who hoped for reform. Daley kept O'Connor on, earning his loyalty. But O'Connor was never in any position to reform, or even control, the police force. The day to day management of the department was conducted by the seven aged and canny assistants in his office who took their orders from the politicians while O'Connor went through the empty motions of being in charge.

A few days after the scandal broke, Daley fired O'Connor as chief and returned him to duty as an ordinary captain. He rationalized the move by telling intimates, "Tim was always telling me how he went home at night and watched TV instead of running around and getting into trouble. I should have asked him why he wasn't running around checking on his policemen at night instead of sitting home watching TV." Of course, O'Connor could have answered such a question with: "If I rock the boat, you will throw me over the side."

Daley knew that firing O'Connor and replacing him with somebody from within the department wasn't enough. Another department-bred chief would probably be as powerless as O'Connor and without credibility. Something big and dramatic was needed to counter the lingering impact of the scandal. And linger it would. The investigation would drag on, then the trials of the policemen, and there was no way of knowing how many more people it would involve. If he didn't do something, it could ruin things in November when state, national, and county elections were being held. Adamowski would be reelected easily, and four more years of his muckraking and scatter-gun prosecution could ruin the Machine.

The next police chief had to be someone from outside Chicago, someone impeccable, expert, and entirely unlike a Chicago policeman. If reforms couldn't be instituted quickly, a new image could be projected, and in politics that is what counts.

Daley checked with several outside experts in law enforcement, and they told him that the top man in the field was a professor at the University of California, head of its criminology department, Orlando W. Wilson. He was the man who wrote the books that progressive police departments read to get the answers.

Wilson sounded like the man, but Daley couldn't offer him the job because anybody he handpicked wouldn't be trusted. He had made up his mind to appoint a nonpolitical committee of outside experts and prominent private citizens. They would interview applicants and they would recommend a man to him. That would help convince the public that he was sincere about reform, that he was willing to give up his prerogatives for the sake of civic betterment.

So Daley's problem was how to hire the man he wanted while making it appear that a committee was doing it. If he left it all up to the committee, Wilson might not even apply. And if he applied, he might not get it. Police chiefs from all over the country were going to be trying for the job. But Daley had a plan.

He sent one of his aides to California to ask Wilson to be chairman of the committee and to look him over. The aide reported to Daley that he was a perfect choice. In a city that saw a cop as a pot-bellied, loud-mouthed, crude, lumbering lout, Wilson would be a complete reversal—tall, lean, calm, a tweedy man who spoke in deliberate, measured sentences. He gave the impression of weighing every thought and utterance with great care. And he was the creator of a new police jargon. Where a Chicago cop would say, "We got a beef and we went in and pinched him, and he took a poke at my partner so I put him down with my billy," Wilson would teach the men to say, "The officers responded to a citizen's complaint and upon arriving at the scene observed that the subject was in the process of committing a crime. The officers placed him under arrest, whereupon he offered resistance and was subdued with necessary force." Daley's determination to hire him was strengthened.

The key was the committee. And the key man on the committee was William McFetridge, Daley's trusted friend and labor leader. Throughout his career, Daley would appoint many similar committees, sparkling with civic and professional leaders—and always including one man who was known to be "Daley's man," nudging the committees toward Daley's wants. McFetridge was "Daley's man" on the police committee.

Wilson came to Chicago and the committee began its hearings. That, in itself, furthered Daley's aim. The committee got coverage by the news media equal to the developments of the scandals, and Daley used the committee for all it was worth. His press conferences were a torrent of confidence that the best man would soon be found, that the new man would be free of political ties, shielded from outside pressures. In the past he had always said that

O'Connor enjoyed such freedoms. For several weeks the applicants went before the committee, presented their credentials, were interviewed on their plans for reform. The suspense mounted and conjecturing on who the new chief would be became the community conversation piece.

When all the applicants had been interviewed, the committee began its deliberations. The choice was difficult. Many were impressive, but no one man had been so outstanding that he towered over the others. That made the committee's job difficult, but it made McFetridge's job easier. At the right moment, when they were tired of the sifting, narrowing process, McFetridge said, "Why don't we select our own chairman?"

Of course. Why not Wilson? He was sitting as chairman because he was the outstanding law enforcement expert in the country, and that was the man the committee was supposed to find. And with Wilson sitting right there, chuckling modestly, who was going to say otherwise? Besides, everybody on the committee knew that McFetridge was Daley's man, and it would never hurt to be on the right side of the mayor.

Wilson held out for two days. Because he was an expert, he knew about Chicago's police-politician relationships. As he said later, "This situation may be the greatest challenge confronting law enforcement in the United States today, perhaps in the world." He wanted a guarantee of independence in the form of a three-year no-strings contract and a salary more than double that paid him by the university.

Daley had no choice. He had decided on reform. Losing the Police Department as a political appendage might be painful, but it had to be done to save the Machine. He gave Wilson everything he asked for. On a Sunday afternoon in late February, they shook on it, and the next day Daley announced the surprising choice at a City Hall press conference. Because it was Washington's birthday, there was little fresh news available, and Wilson's appointment even made the front page of the *New York Times.* It was the first pleasant day Daley had had in the six weeks since the scandal began, posing for pictures with Wilson, giving assurances that Wilson would be given all the help needed to bring goodness and purity to the Police Department.

Wilson took over and the transformation of the Police Department began. But an even more amazing transformation was already underway. Daley, who had been content to allow the Police Department to run wild for five years, had become Daley, the zealous reformer of same. The scandal was off page one, and it was replaced by Daley vowing to whip the council into passing needed reform ordinances; Daley promising Wilson as much money as he needed for higher salaries and modern equipment; Daley going to Springfield to fight for new police legislation; Daley protecting Wilson from the reactionary political forces.

"I will give him all the cooperation he needs to make the Chicago Police Department the finest in the nation," said Daley in one story. And the headline of another was: "Church Group Behind Daley and Wilson." It was Daley and Wilson, all of a sudden.

Some of Wilson's plans were more than the ward bosses could suffer in silence. He was going to close down about half the stations, centralize operations, shatter the old ward boundaries of police districts. This meant that the ward bosses lost their right to name their police captains. He threw out all the old civil service promotion lists and held legitimate tests. Men who were mired in the patrolman ranks jumped two or three ranks almost overnight. Old-timers quit rather than face a life of honest work. He fired all seven of the politically influential deputy commissioners who had surrounded O'Connor. Some ward bosses said they wouldn't take it. Reform was nice, but he was ruining their Police Department.

But there was Daley to shield Wilson, beating down the evil ward bosses who opposed the Daley-Wilson reform. The editor of one paper wrote: "Fortunately, Mayor Daley remains firm in his determination that Wilson will be given a free hand in cleaning up the mess." The writer didn't note that Daley had always given his cops a free hand to fill their pockets.

Another columnist wrote: "I think now, more than ever, that Wilson will succeed. And he is working for a mayor whose word is good." His word? How good was it when he used to say that critics of his corrupt Police Department were liars?

When Daley's back wasn't being pummeled by the editorial writers and columnists, stories of his Cyrano-like thrusts against the enemy were being headlined: "Mayor Daley said Friday that he will go to Springfield with or without an invitation if any legislation is submitted affecting the Chicago Police Department. 'I will go there in the interests of 4,000,000 people.' "

It was a triumph in public relations. Wilson proved to be one of Daley's greatest political assets. His professional manner and dry wit made him a natural for the TV talk shows and interviews. Even before any changes were made in the police force, his presence implied great change. And five years after Daley first made it a campaign promise, the police chief finally moved his office out of City Hall and into police headquarters.

"The amazing thing about the police scandal," Alderman Simon has said, "is the way Daley turned it to his own advantage. He'd been in office five years and he knew from a lifetime of experience that the cops were on the take. Then when the scandal hit, instead of Daley being held responsible, he fired O'Connor, Wilson came in, and Daley was the guy who reformed it. Anybody else would have been raked over the coals—Lindsay is always blamed for what happens in New York—but Daley wound up being treated like a hero and a reformer. He turned it to his own advantage."

Daley's miracle came just in time. The elections were coming up in November. At the Democratic Convention, he had delivered the Illinois delegation to John Kennedy after coldly rejecting Adlai Stevenson's last-minute plea for support from his home state and was in the position to enhance his budding reputation as a "king maker" by bringing Illinois in for Kennedy. As always, however, the Machine's priority was the local ticket. Adamowski had to be beaten and the state's attorney's office placed in safe hands.

Arvey had taught him that when the situation is critical, find a shiny new face. His candidate for state's attorney was Daniel Ward, dean of a law school and political newcomer. The rest of his ticket had superficial luster, all good-looking, erudite, and most of them sons of former party chiefs.

It was a "must" election and the Machine came through and won, sweeping all state and county offices and bringing in Illinois for Kennedy by a nervous ten thousand votes. But how it won became a subject of debate, as well as lawsuits and fistfights.

The day after the election, Adamowski, who had lost by a county-wide margin of only twenty-five thousand votes, charged that "Daley has stolen the White House" and the Republicans demanded a recheck, which they were legally entitled to, so long as they paid the cost.

Daley's election board soberly announced that it would be glad to conduct a recheck, and it began, one precinct a day. At that pace, they would complete the recheck in twenty years. When they stopped stalling, it became obvious that if they hadn't stolen the White House, or more likely, Adamowski's office, it wasn't because they hadn't tried.

In nine hundred precincts in which paper ballots were still used, the recheck caused a switch of ten thousand votes, narrowing Adamowski's margin of defeat to fifteen thousand.

Nixon gained very little in the nine hundred precincts, showing clearly that the Machine was more concerned with beating Adamowski than electing Kennedy. With nothing to gain for Nixon, the Republicans lost interest, leaving Adamowski with the cost of the recheck—more than six hundred dollars a day. He didn't have the money, so he had to give it up.

Daley's election board members looked innocent throughout the limited recheck and blamed it all on human error, brought on by the fatigue of a long day and evening in the polling place. They didn't explain why the human errors consistently benefited Democrats.

The fraud was so obvious that Daley had to permit a special prosecutor to be appointed to investigate. More than six hundred polling-place workers and precinct captains were brought to trial. To assure that the fix wouldn't be put in by a local judge, a downstate judge was called in to hear the cases. The downstate judge turned out to be a faithful organization Democrat, and later most of the charges were wiped out.

The vote-fraud furor lasted many weeks after the election, but Daley wasn't flustered. The Republicans and the papers, forgetting for the moment that Daley had been elevated by them to the rank of reformer-leader, could sputter all they wanted about low-down Machine vote stealing. He had pulled it off. Kennedy had been elected. Adamowski could go back to practicing law and brooding. His man Otto Kerner, obedient and faithful, was in the governor's mansion, which meant thousands of state jobs would be filled by party men. Hundreds more would be regained in Cook County offices, all controlled by the Machine. When he boarded the Inauguration Special with his family and one thousand other Democrats to go to Washington, he was the most powerful political leader in Illinois' history, and, with the single exception of the president, the most powerful politician in the country.

He would assert this power, however, in a way limited only to Chicago. His interest in the workings of Washington was confined primarily to obtaining federal money and laws for Chicago. His influence with the Democratic White House would be used to bend federal guidelines on the spending of such money. The poverty program, for instance, often placed in the hands of private agencies and grassroots organizations in other cities, would never be out of his control in Chicago, regardless of what the federal laws might demand. His power was based on his ability to deliver the Cook County vote. His ties with the White House would be used to maintain that strength. From the day Kennedy took office, to the time Lyndon Johnson refused to run for another term, speculation that Daley might come to Washington as a cabinet member continued. But in Chicago such a possibility was never taken seriously. Daley preferred running his own city to taking orders from the man running the country.

In Washington, he was greeted as a "king maker." Kennedy himself had said Daley had won it for him. On Inauguration Day, Daley was standing in a crowded ballroom for a governor's reception when the secret service bulled in to clear a path, shoving Sis one way and sending Daley staggering the other. Kennedy spotted him, stopped, and grabbed his hand. "Where are you staying?" asked the president. "The Sheraton Park, and I'll give you a call," said Daley of Bridgeport. "I'll give you a call," said the president of the United States. He did, and the family went to the White House and posed for a group picture with Kennedy. "We were the first family invited to the White House," Daley boasted when he came out.

The picture was taken almost a year to the day after Daley, his face sagging and his hand shaking, formed a committee to find a new police chief because his world was crashing around his ears. In one year he had changed it all and was even more powerful. It just showed what hard work and imagination could do. That, plus a few thousand election workers who were prone to "human error."

With the elections behind him, Daley returned to the task of making life better in his city, a city of neighborhoods, by plotting the elimination of one of the city's oldest and most colorful neighborhoods.

Known as the "Valley," it was only a mile or two southwest of the Loop, and had been the original home of the city's Italians. In its early days, it had been a dangerous place for a non-Italian to show his face. Most of the immigrant Mafiosi had settled there, and it produced their home-grown successors. But by the 1960s it was a quieter place and the residents were fighting to keep it alive. The best Italian restaurants, the stores that sold the cheeses and the spices, and the sense of home were there. Much of the property was very old and run down, but the people had reversed the deterioration and the neighborhood was improving.

City Hall had promised that urban renewal would be used to help restore and stabilize the community. Some of the oldest blocks had already been torn down with the promise that new, moderate-income housing would be put up. The people believed, and many of them were putting money into improving their homes, modernizing their small businesses. The Chicago archdiocese had built a big, new, modern school. The future looked good for the Valley, and at a time when people were rushing to the suburbs, it looked good for the city to have a neighborhood get better instead of worse. Few were.

The people of the Valley didn't know that City Hall had made another decision. The Valley had to go. Daley needed a site for a University of Illinois campus, and the Italian community was it. He had tried to get the various railroads to agree on a common terminal, thus freeing some of their land, but the railroads were looking for a better financial deal than the merger could give them. There also was the area due west of the Loop, including the eyesore Skid Row and some small industry, and it would have been perfect. But the real estate interests already had their eye on it for big high-rise developments, and the Valley could never be grabbed for that purpose. Other alternatives were rejected, some because they were too far from the Loop, others because they were in black areas.

While the people in the neighborhood spent and rebuilt, City Hall proceeded with its secret plan. Quietly, the power groups in the community were persuaded to go along. The archdiocese, which had its big new school and its churches, agreed. The ward boss and party hacks were given their orders. That took care of the established leaders of any community resistance. There was nobody to lead them but themselves. Only then was the plan announced.

Despite the careful groundwork, Daley found himself facing the first community uprising of his administration. Later there would be many more, but the Valley was the first.

The people at first were stunned and disorganized. The neighborhood's sense of betrayal was heightened by the fact that they had been a loyal Machine ward. They poured out more Democratic votes than Daley's own neighborhood. But they found grassroots leaders who were far superior to the slobs they had been electing over the years. They organized protest meetings, marches, and sit-ins, tame by contemporary standards, but a novelty in the preriot era. Florence Scala, a young housewife with a college background, emerged as their spokesman and led them to City Hall for their first meeting with Daley.

"It was on St. Valentine's Day and he gave us the happy Valentine's Day bit. The women pleaded with him, 'Don't take our homes away, please, let us keep our homes.' He kept saying that he'd give us new housing nearby if we gave up our own. We tried to talk about our planning and he kept talking about all the new housing he was going to build for us right nearby, right in the same area. When we finished, he was still reassuring us and acting friendly. That's when I told him: 'I'm going to fight you on this.' His face got so cold and the smile just disappeared.

"The next time we saw him was after the City Council approved our neighborhood as the site. That night some kids threw a rock through the alderman's office window and some other kids went to Daley's neighborhood with an effigy doused in ketchup that they threw in front of his house. The day after it happened, we went into his office for another meeting and I apologized for the incident at his home and said we had nothing to do with it and disapproved of that kind of thing. He was very gracious. He said: 'I realize that; that's all right, I realize that.' When the press was admitted he changed completely. Somebody asked about the effigy and he got very tough and said things like, 'Nobody gets tough with me, I know how to handle myself, I know how to protect myself. I come from the kind of neighborhood where we know how to protect ourselves.' It was obvious that he was trying to humiliate us in front of the press, and on television that night, it came out that way, that we were responsible for his home being bothered and he was telling us off good.

"It was never possible to get him to be honest with us. Sometimes he'd say that he had nothing to do with the decision, that it had been made by the university trustees and that we should be talking to them. Then we'd go to see the trustees and they'd sit there with their mouths open. Then sometimes he'd get very tough and tell us: 'I won't talk to you. Where's your lawyer. I'll talk to your lawyer.'

"Only once did he show a flicker of being a person. He came out of his office one night. It was after five o'clock and most of the people in City Hall had gone home. Four of us were sitting in outside of his office. He went past us toward the elevator, then he walked back and said: 'How long are you going to sit there?' I said, 'All night.' He looked at us then he said: 'C'mon, I'll buy you a cup of coffee.' I said no, so he shrugged and left. After he went down, I realized that maybe we should have gone with him.

"About ten thousand people were moved out, not counting the ones who owned small businesses along the edge.

Some of them went out to the Austin neighborhood where they've got new problems now with the neighborhood changing racially. Others went out to Cicero. All that housing they were going to put up for us? I think they put up forty-four units in one place, and about fifty units in another. And most of it was too high-priced for the people who lived there."

Despite the definite need for a campus site, the way it was handled didn't set too well with people in other neighborhoods who could identify with the hard-pressed residents of the Valley. Downtown, the adulation of projects and new buildings was fervent as ever. But in the neighborhoods, where people owned their small bungalows and two-flats, the big downtown projects meant only one thing to them—taxes—and taxes were going up. The real estate tax had risen faster in Chicago than in any other major city during the 1950s, some of the biggest increases coinciding with money-wasting scandals.

Just when the police scandal faded away, another emerged at a political playpen called the Sanitary District, an agency responsible for the city's sewage disposal. It is considered an engineering marvel, but the wonder of the place was the way the people who ran it figured out new and better ways to make money off inflated contracts, peddling of jobs, and other knavery.

Once again, Daley had to appoint a citizen's committee to bring in a reform administrator, and once again he was praised for his civic goodness. His Machine hacks had long been looting the Sanitary District, but that was overlooked.

The voters weren't overlooking it, however, and in 1962 when he put forth a $66-million bond issue referendum for public works, it was soundly defeated. Suddenly Daley had a taxpayer's revolt on his hands, with his own re-election just over the horizon. His opponent was going to be the irrepressible Ben Adamowski, this time armed with a wealth of campaign issues—scandals, waste, and high taxes.

The city's Republicans, including the business interests, would have preferred that no one run against Daley, but Adamowski forced himself on them. He thought that after four years of scandal, Daley could be beaten. But before

Adamowski could get his campaign underway, Daley threw him off balance by going on the offensive.

State's Attorney Ward had dug up some contingency-fund records left behind by Adamowski. Precise accounting wasn't required in the contingency fund, since it was to be used for such things as paying off secret informants in criminal cases, but there were indications that some of the money might have been used in Adamowski's 1960 campaign. Ward didn't have enough evidence to go to court, or even make a believable threat, but he told Daley about it. As usual, Daley's policy was to never attack his opponent personally. So the material was leaked to the press. That way, the press could attack his opponent personally. Adamowski found himself starting his campaign on the defensive, trying to explain his old contingency fund, while Daley looked pious. Daley was asked rather gently by the newspapers how he spent his own $50,000-a-year contingency fund, but under the city ordinance, he didn't have to account for it even as casually as Adamowski did his.

When he finally recovered from the faltering start, Adamowski was unable to convince the news media that Daley was in any way responsible for the scandals of his administration. To the contrary, Daley was eulogized as the great reformer. Ignored was the fact that he instituted reforms only after his people got caught.

At about the same time, a black alderman and ward committeeman, Ben Lewis, was handcuffed to a chair in his office and shot three times in the head. Nobody knew who killed him and his murder was never solved. Lewis had been the ward boss in name only, because white precinct captains ran the organization, including him. The police questioned policy-wheel operators, gamblers, and hoodlums of all kinds. Crime syndicate names came up. It was an enlightening civics lesson, and a reminder of the kind of people who kept the Machine chugging along.

An alderman's being murdered in Mafia style didn't improve Daley's four-year record, but about the time the killing took place, *Time* magazine put Daley on the cover and lavished him with praise, while dismissing Adamowski in one sentence. The city's papers pointed at the *Time* article as evidence of their own political perception.

Adamowski's biggest problem was getting campaign money from the Republican leaders.

"I couldn't get through at all to the businessmen. I was trying to get at least enough money for the precinct work. I knew that without precinct money, they'd beat me. We don't have the patronage jobs, so if a precinct worker is going to take a day off from work, you have to give him something and help cover his expenses. Without the precinct money, you don't have poll watchers and they can get away with anything. But the businessmen didn't help. Do you know what I got from Chuck Percy? He sent me a check for one hundred dollars. How about that, from the chairman of Bell and Howell, one hundred dollars. Most of my contributions came from small people, tens and twenties, from people in the neighborhoods."

It was a strange reversal of the traditional roles—the downtown businessmen sending their checks to the Democrats, while the working class contributed to the Republicans. The neighborhood people sent money, but they had to be careful of more visible signs of support. The owner of a small restaurant at Division and Ashland, the heart of the city's Polish neighborhood, put up a big Adamowski sign. The day it went up the precinct captain came around and said, "How come the sign Harry?" "Ben's a friend of mine," the restaurant owner said. "Ben's a nice guy Harry, but that's a pretty big sign. I'd appreciate it if you'd take it down." "No, it's staying up."

The next day the captain came back. "Look, I'm the precinct captain. Is there anything wrong, any problem, anything I can help you with?" Harry said no. "Then why don't you take it down. You know how this looks in my job." Harry wouldn't budge. The sign stayed up.

On the third day, the city building inspectors came. The plumbing improvements alone cost Harry $2,100.

That kind of vindictiveness wasn't necessary in 1959 with Sheehan, but this time Daley was running scared. The lost bond issue had told him something. He campaigned hard and just before election, President Kennedy came in for a dedication at O'Hare Airport.

When the polls closed on election night, Democratic headquarters had an uncharacteristic tension. Daley's sons hustled into his office with the early precinct returns and they weren't good. The home-owner neighborhoods were going for Adamowski. The tax revolt was showing itself. In Adamowski's headquarters, the atmosphere was one of excitement, almost jubilation. Adamowski posed for a picture and said: "I think you just photographed the next mayor of Chicago." That was at about eight o'clock. By nine he was stony-faced and Democratic headquarters was relaxing. Dawson's wards had come in. So had the Twenty-fourth Ward, which hadn't suffered politically by the murder of its Alderman Lewis. Daley was in.

It wasn't a landslide to compare with 1959, when he got seventy-one percent of the vote and won by 466,000. Against Adamowski it dropped to fifty-five percent and a margin of 138,000. But it was enough to send everybody home happy. After four years that would have ruined any other mayor, fifty-five percent was, in fact, quite comfortable.

Later, when they sat down and went over the figures closely, they found an interesting pattern. Adamowski had received fifty-one percent of the votes, cast by white persons. But the enormous black vote had given Daley his victory. The people who were trapped in the ghetto slums and the nightmarish public housing projects, the people who had the worst school system and were most often degraded by the Police Department, the people who received the fewest campaign promises and who were ignored as part of the campaign trail, had given him his third term. They had done it quietly, asking for nothing in return. Exactly what they got.

Chapter VII

KUNSTLER: Now, Mayor Daley, on April 15th,
1968, did you order your Police Department
to shoot to kill and to shoot to maim black
people in the city of Chicago?

FORAN: Your honor, I object to the question
on the ground that it is leading, suggestive,
immaterial, irrelevant and clearly improper.

John Walsh, high school English teacher, civil rights
worker, pacifist, amateur actor, and lawyer, had an idea.

"I believed that it was only proper that a Negro should
live on the same street near the home of the mayor of the
city of Chicago."

Stated that way, simply and directly, there was nothing
revolutionary about his idea. Why not a Negro on the
same street, near the mayor's home? It was 1964, the civil
rights movement was sweeping across the land, all the way
into the halls of Congress. First Kennedy, then Johnson,
had placed themselves firmly on the side of fair play and
integration. Daley, in his public utterances, was with them.

Beyond that, Daley himself had said, more than once,
that Chicago wasn't segregated. Way back in 1956,
Eleanor Roosevelt had suggested on a TV show that northern cities desegregate to set an example for the rest of the

nation, particularly the South. The next day, Daley was asked what he thought of Mrs. Roosevelt's proposal, and he said:

"We believe that we do not have segregation in Chicago. Here we recognize every man, regardless of race, nationalistic origin, or creed, and they are all entitled to their rights as provided in the United States Constitution and the Constitution of Illinois."

That took care of integration until the following year, when Edwin Berry, the new executive director of the Chicago Urban League, charged that Chicago was the most residentially segregated city in the United States, a place where "a Negro dare not step outside the environs of his race."

Daley answered: "I don't believe Chicago is as bad as some people say it is. We are making progress in race relations."

By 1963, he still believed in the racial progress of his city, telling the NAACP that "there are no ghettos in Chicago." He was booed off the Grant Park bandshell by civil rights activists a couple of days later, but he didn't change his mind about the absence of ghettos.

That being the case, John Walsh set about proving that the mayor was right. If there was no segregation in Chicago, a Negro in his neighborhood shouldn't attract attention.

Walsh and a friend with money quietly bought a small frame house containing three apartments at 3309 Lowe, a block and a half from the mayor's pink bungalow. Their plan was to rent one of the flats to Negroes.

"Our biggest problem was finding somebody willing to move in. Bridgeport's reputation was well known among Negroes. It was the kind of neighborhood they wouldn't walk through at night, and during the day it wasn't a good idea either. We finally found a young couple and they got as far as the front door. Then the key jammed and they panicked. They turned right around and left. We found two other couples and each time they backed out at the last minute."

Years of conditioning were at work. Few blacks even thought about moving into Bridgeport or any other white neighborhood. Those who tried found that the real estate offices in the neighborhoods didn't have anything available. The only way out of the ghetto was to the next block, across the border, where the panic peddling real estate men worked on the frightened working-class whites, sending them fleeing and selling their homes cheap, which the real estate men promptly bought and sold at inflated prices to the Negroes. The Negro couldn't get out of the black ghetto. He merely extended it another fraction of an inch on the city map. The few who made the brave jump deep into white neighborhoods learned that it wasn't worth the dangers. Their homes were burned or bombed. In 1952, Governor Stevenson had to call out the national guard when the old Capone suburb of Cicero went beserk and stormed a house bought by a black man.

Walsh kept looking, and he finally found two college students who said they'd move in. On a Friday in October they arrived with their belongings. Integration had come to Bridgeport for the first time in its hundred-year history.

The old Daley neighbors didn't take kindly to the new Daley neighbors, and over the weekend angry crowds drifted up and down Lowe Avenue. They tried to talk to Daley, but the police kept them away from his house, so they went back to the three-flat and chanted hate messages at the two nervous young black men. Rocks crashed through the window and bottles broke against the doors.

By Monday night, it was a junior-sized riot, with at least four hundred people from the neighborhood fighting with the police, trying to storm the building, a dozen getting arrested, and four policemen being injured.

Through it all, Daley stayed out of sight. He didn't poke his nose out of his house once and didn't say anything about the battle being fought 350 feet away. The news media cooperated by virtually ignoring the incident.

Behind the scenes, however, the Eleventh Ward Regular Democratic Organization was working out a way to settle the matter.

While the two students were at school, the police went in the flat and carried their belongings to the corner police station. People from the neighborhood rushed in and threw the place up for grabs, smearing excrement on the walls.

The real estate man who handled the move-in was summoned by the ward organization and told what to do.

He listened because real estate licenses are under the control of the mayor of the city of Chicago. They told him that the two black youths were no longer tenants in the building; that two white men from the neighborhood were going to move in and were going to be given a long, unbreakable lease for the apartment, and that it was all going to happen immediately. The lease was drawn up, signed, and the two white tenants moved in. The jubilant crowd joined them in the apartment for a celebration and to help clean up the mess.

When the black students got back to Bridgeport that night, they were taken to the police station, given their belongings and told that they no longer lived in Bridgeport. When John Walsh got home that night, he found that he owned a three-flat with white tenants and all of them had unbreakable leases. Walsh soon sold the building. If he hadn't, he would have gone broke trying to meet the city building department's demands for improvements. Chicago has one of the nation's strictest building codes. Although rarely enforced, it provides City Hall with a powerful club over property owners.

"I proved that Daley was guilty of passive hypocrisy," Walsh said. "He could have prevented all the trouble. He could have controlled his own people. And he knew what we were doing. Weeks before we moved anybody in, I told the city's Human Relations Commission about my plan. I promised them that we would rent only one apartment to Negroes and that all the income from the property would be used for improving it. Instead, they let it happen, they let the people in the neighborhood drive us out. And Daley didn't lift a finger."

It would have been a greater surprise if Daley had reacted in any other way, such as walking down the street to shake hands and welcome the black youths to Bridgeport. Although he parroted the national liberal policies of the Democratic party, civil rights and human equality were things in the planks of party platforms, the words of legislation. His first eight years in office did little to change the way of black life in Chicago—slums, welfare checks, and don't forget to vote.

The blacks were crammed into two ghettos, the old one on the South Side, and the new one on the near West

Side. They weren't Daley's concern. If problems arose, Dawson or one of his men were consulted. They were his straw bosses, harvesting the rich black vote for him.

Containing the Negro was unspoken city policy. Even expressways were planned as man-made barriers, the unofficial borders. The Dan Ryan, for instance, was shifted several blocks during the planning stage to make one of the ghetto walls. Proposals to scatter public housing, thus breaking the segregation pattern, were killed by City Hall. The city's rule was that no public housing could go into a ward without the alderman's consent. Housing for the aged was kept out of white wards because it might attract some old Negroes.

The suburbs were no better, and maybe worse. In theory, suburbanites should have been more receptive to integration because they were wealthier, better educated, and would feel less threatened with the mass of Negroes so far away. But in 1960, when a liberal real estate developer tried to put up an expensive, integrated housing development in the gracious North Shore suburb of Deerfield, a community where nobody would say "nigger" at a cocktail party and where many of the residents sent yearly checks to the NAACP, the town condemned the land for use as a park.

If Chicago's slums weren't the worst in the nation, they were in the running. Slum housing was a big business for white real estate men. Six apartments could be carved into eighteen and the rents jacked up because it was a seller's market. It was illegal, but the building department was happy to be bought off. The rents were almost all profit, because the slum owners didn't maintain the buildings. That was illegal, too, but the inspectors got theirs. Everybody was in the slum business. Universities owned them, and so did churches, fraternal organizations, and prominent establishment types. They avoided public embarrassment because Illinois is one of the few states in which the hidden land trust, concealing the real owners of property, is legal.

Outsiders paid attention to slum conditions only when they burned and a black family died. A fuss would be made about forcing slum owners to improve their property, but the real evil—segregated, restrictive housing—was never attacked. The official City Hall myth was that Negroes didn't really want to go live in white neighborhoods. Daley's housing director once said, "There is 'voluntary' segregation in Chicago in which members of a minority group live together because of cultural, social and other ties." Hungry people who slept five in a bed, not counting rats, and saw the sky through the holes in their roof, might not have agreed that it was a "voluntary" arrangement.

Stuffed in his ghetto, the Negro wasn't even allowed to suffer in privacy. He was too good a mark for the exploiter. In the early 1950s, the Mafia murdered its way into control of the lucrative numbers wheels, taking away the black's only home-grown racket. Most small and large businesses in the black ghettos were owned by outside whites. Cheap merchandise was overpriced to start with, then sold on time with fantastic interest. Everything cost more in the ghettos, from gas for the car, to the car itself, to the food on the grocery store shelf.

Politically, the Negro was even more exploitable. In the South he didn't vote. In Chicago he could vote for the Democrat of his choice. The Machine's precinct captains would go right into the voting booth with him to make sure he voted properly. The major weapon was the threat. Negroes were warned that they would lose their welfare check, their public housing apartment, their menial job, if they didn't vote Democratic. Dawson ran everything on the South Side, but on the West Side, where most of the new arrivals from the South settled, they didn't even have black politicians exploiting them. The white officeholders and ward bosses remained after the white constituents fled.

If the Negro was equal in the eyes of the law, the men wearing badges needed glasses. Police were brutal in a casual, offhand way. A black might be picked up as a suspect on a Friday night, tossed in a cell, and kept around for two, three, or four days, while the detectives decided whether to charge him with something. If it turned out he wasn't the right man, they'd charge him with disorderly conduct so he could be let out on bond, if he had it. If not he might spend a few more days waiting to go to court. Suspects were beaten into confessions, but white courts and a white news media were indifferent. It improved slightly under Orlando Wilson's reorganization, but not enough to turn Negroes into law-and-order buffs.

Problems of black life, and death, were seldom discussed by politicians of either party. They spent most of their time in empty-headed debate over the number of black babies being born to sex-crazed welfare mothers and able-bodied, sex-crazed black men who chose a life of idleness. To hear the politicians tell it, life in the ghetto was a whirl of passion, welfare checks, and liquor.

They reflected the white population's attitude. Most Chicago whites hated blacks. The only genuine difference between a southern white and a Chicago white was in their accent. Blacks could walk through a white neighborhood, but only if he looked like he was going to the nearest bus stop or a restaurant to wash dishes. A black who went into a tavern in a white neighborhood might get a drink, or he might be hit. If he got a drink, chances are the bartender would charge him a dollar extra then smash his empty glass into the garbage can. During the 1950s, most restaurants wouldn't seat blacks, most hotels wouldn't accommodate them, and the Loop was considered off limits. As a rule, South Side whites hated blacks more than North Side whites did, because the blacks were closer.

That's the way it was in 1956, when Daley said there was no segregation in Chicago, and that's the way it was at the beginning of his third term, when he said there were no ghettos in Chicago. In a muddleheaded way, he may have even meant it.

To Daley, the blacks were merely going through the same onward and upward process of all other ethnic groups, huddling together and waiting for their chance to move up the American ladder. The Irish had done it and so had the other European groups. They put in their time in rickety neighborhoods then moved on. Daley was a firm believer in the bootstrap theory.

A nun who did social work on the West Side once went to see him about the foul living conditions. She wanted to tell him about the black children who were dying of lead poisoning because they ate flaking plaster in the crumbling slums, about the infant mortality rate as high

as in Ceylon, about the feeble housing-code enforcement
and his inspectors taking bribes, about the lack of playlots
and ball fields, the absence of a real urban renewal
program and the other evils in the fifty-block neighborhood.

She thought that because she was a nun he might pay
more attention to her than he did to the black activists
who were distrusted by City Hall. But she barely began to
speak her piece when he cut in.

"Sister, you and I come from the same background . . .
grandparents came here with nothing . . . took care of their
houses . . . look at Bridgeport . . . houses as old as on the
West Side but the people took care of them, worked hard,
kept the neighborhood clean, looked after their children
. . . let me tell you something about those people . . .
should lift themselves up by their bootstraps like our
grandparents did . . . take care of their children . . .
work hard . . . take care of their houses."

The nun tried to explain some of the differences between
being an Irish immigrant, some of whom went on the
police force the same week they got to Chicago, and being
a black man, some of whom were thrown into a cell the
same day they got to Chicago. She tried to get into the
matter of trade unions. His own father had been in the
sheet-metal-workers' union forty years earlier, but blacks
were still kept out. She barely got a word in. Every time
she tried, he came back with more of the bootstrap
theory. She gave up and left.

The fears common to his generation and background
were in him, too. A priest who knows him well said, "I
think that if one of his kids had ever dated a Negro, it
would have sickened him." Not surprisingly, the rest of his
family appears to have shared his views. When two of his
sons were in their late teens, they saw a friend waiting for
a bus on South Halsted Street. They honked and offered
him a lift. He got in and said they could drop him at the
Thirty-fifth Street elevated station, which is in the black
area. One of them said, "We'd better not drop you there.
We'll take you downtown," which they did, driving four
miles to white safety.

When the youngest son, William, was a senior in high
school, he had difficulties with a Jesuit teacher-priest who

used a contemporary study of racial problems in the United States as a text book. The book *Crisis in Black and White*, by Charles E. Silberman, not only put Daley in a dim light, but put the race question in militant terms.

Mrs. Daley had complained about the book several times to the principal, also a Jesuit, and had threatened to yank William out of the school. "That book is just a lot of stuff he got out of the papers," she said. Finally, during a test, William launched a diatribe against the book and was docked for not answering the question.

Most of the young men in the class shared his opinions and did badly on the tests, so the young Jesuit teacher asked the parents to come in for a conference. The Daleys, however, had a private interview.

When the teacher explained that William had done badly on the tests, Daley snapped, "Half of that book is false." The teacher sarcastically invited Daley to lecture the class on which half of the book was false, but Daley ignored that, saying, "We thought this was a religious class." The teacher told him that it was a religious class, dealing with racial problems. Daley said, "When we were in school, we weren't just supposed to parrot back what a book said. We were asked our opinions."

The Jesuit said that the students were given ample opportunity to discuss the book and register disagreement, but the test had been given to measure their ability to absorb the material being discussed. Daley appeared unimpressed, and as he left, he stared coldly at the priest and said, "I'll make sure he reads those books and gives the material right back at you the way it is." Mrs. Daley nodded throughout.

Besides bootstraps and fear, it was politically wise to keep the black where he was. Concentrated, the black vote was easily controlled. But if open housing became a reality the black vote bloc would be lost, the white voter would be outraged by the presence of the black, and the Machine would collapse.

There was no reason, personal or political, for Daley to have done anything more during his first two terms. So he didn't. The black had been docile, asking for less than any other group, and obedient, voting more consistently

Democratic than any other group. It was a pleasant political one-way street.

But when Daley's third term began, the black silence ended. The "invisible man" of Ralph Ellison's novel materialized. As Daley was jeered off the bandshell in Grant Park in the summer of 1963, his face swollen with anger, he knew something new was starting to happen in Chicago.

The blacks, led by the Woodlawn Organization, a group founded by Saul Alinsky, began by coming downtown with picket signs and demanding better schools. That was the first issue in the Chicago civil rights movement. Even more important than the dumps they lived in were the dumps their kids were not being educated in. Black children were on double shifts. The ghetto schools were crowded, while hundreds of classrooms stood empty in white schools. The Daley-appointed school board finally acknowledged that the overcrowding existed, and it moved to ease the problem by bringing in trailer classrooms and converting old buildings and warehouses into schools, thus neatly side-stepping integration. Rather than allow black kids to travel to the empty rooms in white schools, the solution was to add classrooms in the ghetto schools.

The mobile classrooms were promptly dubbed "Willis Wagons," after School Superintendent Benjamin Willis, and he became the chief target of the civil rights groups that were springing up. Willis was a perfect choice: arrogant, authoritarian, unyielding, capable of offending and alienating anyone. He bullied the school board which, in theory, employed him, and he chose to ignore the black protest. The more experienced civil rights workers were delighted. Nothing can wither a movement faster than a conciliatory, sympathetic adversary. Willis was like a rock.

After the picketing of 1963, the movement accelerated. School boycotts were organized, and tens of thousands of black kids were kept home. The angry outcry from officials and the press was deafening. Never before had they expressed such great concern for the education of little black children as they did when the little black children were kept out of their third-rate schools for a day. There had been no comparable indignation when the black children left elementary school without knowing how to read, or when they graduated from high school barely knowing how to write.

The boycotts were the first solid evidence that the civil rights movement had widespread support among Chicago's Negroes, as well as organization. No longer were they just asking for something. They were demonstrating power. They were demanding—demanding that Willis be fired. Daley did what he had always done when somebody made demands or tried to grab some of his power. He dug in his heels. He refused to consider the firing of Willis, pleading that the school board ran the system and he wouldn't tamper with it.

One of Daley's former aides said there were other valid political reasons for keeping Willis on.

"The more the blacks picked on Willis, the more popular he became among the whites. If Daley gave in, the whites would have been mad. He figured he'd always get the black vote, but the whites had already shown that they'd go for somebody else when they went for Adamowski. Besides, Willis was useful to Daley. If the civil rights people kept after Willis, it kept the heat off Daley."

The distant rumblings of more serious trouble were being felt across the country, but not by Daley. A small riot had broken out in the suburb of Dixmoor in 1964. If a riot could occur in one of the few black suburbs, where living conditions were superior to Chicago's ghetto, it was reasonable to assume that Chicago's day wasn't far off. Daley, however, went on treating the civil rights groups like a minor irritant, while unfurling new plans and programs at his press conferences, none of which meant anything to the frustrated black in the ghettos. He depended on his black aldermen for advice, and they were just as jealous of their own power as he was. They assured him that the new civil rights groups, with initials for names, were nobodies, that they had no followers, there was nothing to worry about, that the blacks in their wards were thrilled with all of the programs Daley was announcing.

In early 1965, Daley and the mayors of other major cities were quietly invited to take part in a secret federal program to chart ways riots could be avoided. Nothing was announced to the public because the White House felt that talking about riot prevention might alarm the public and even provoke riots.

Daley was so confident nothing could happen in Chicago that he rudely rejected the invitation from Washington. He was the only one of eleven mayors invited to the sessions who refused to come. Daley angrily warned a federal official to "keep hands off Chicago." Then he relented slightly, told the federal people that he wouldn't object if they sent someone out to talk to his aides, and finally turned the matter over to a low-level underling, who let it drop. The underling decided that the program was "vague and unnecessary."

Full of confidence, Daley faced his second summer of civil rights activity. But the demonstrations didn't fade away, as his black aldermen had assured him they would. They just went into another part of town. Daley had ignored them when they came downtown, so they went where he couldn't ignore them—out to Bridgeport and the pink bungalow on Lowe Avenue.

The neighborhood was stunned when it looked out of its windows and saw seventy-five sign-waving blacks and white liberals trooping along with Dick Gregory, of all people, in the lead. Gregory, after his success in show business, had turned to civil rights and had become the best known, if not the most effective, of the Chicago leaders.

Bridgeport's reaction was predictable. The second night the marchers showed up, the neighborhood mob grew to almost a thousand. The marchers were showered with eggs and tomatoes, fire crackers and rocks. Women came out of their houses to turn on lawn sprinklers, soaking the marchers as they walked by. The neighborhood echoed with the chants of "Two-four-six-eight, we don't want to integrate," and hundreds of voices joined to sing: "Oh, I wish I was an Alabama trooper, that is what I'd really like to be-ee-ee. Cuz if I was an Alabama trooper, I could kill the niggers legally."

Daley sat in the house, out of sight, but giving orders to the corner police station by phone. Extra police had been brought in, but the Bridgeport mob grew by the minute. It was already three or four times the size of the crowd that had tried to storm John Walsh's black tenants.

Something had to be done, and Daley gave the orders: the police were told to start making arrests.

However, they did not arrest the rock- and egg-throwers, the people who were pushing and shoving at the police lines to get at the handful of peaceful marchers. They arrested the peaceful marchers, put them in paddy wagons, and charged them with disorderly conduct. The police captain at the scene said that it was easier to arrest the marchers for being disorderly because they were peaceful; whereas he did not want to arrest Daley's neighbors for disorderly conduct, because they were disorderly and might fight. So the only way to maintain peace was to lock up those who were peaceful.

Even the nonpicketing civil rights leaders, such as Edwin Berry of the Urban League, were angered by Daley's logic. Berry stormed into Daley's office and berated both Daley and Wilson, telling them, "You are wrong as hell on this." Wilson insisted that it was the best way to avert bloodshed, and Daley, very grim, said nothing while Berry was there. But later, for the white TV audience, he lashed out at the civil rights groups for invading the privacy of his neighbors. Of his chanting, rock-throwing neighbors, he said, "They are fine people, hard-working people. And they have no feelings one way or another about all of this."

This kind of talk brought the anti-Willis marchers back to Bridgeport the very next day, and the next day, and every day that week and the following week. But Bridgeport became calm. Daley sent his precinct captains and other jobholders door-to-door, telling people to stay inside, to ignore Gregory's crowd. None of them were moving in. They were just passing through, so there was nothing to get excited about. The precinct captains reminded them that Daley was more than just their friend and neighbor, he was also the man who signed their City Hall paychecks. They took the advice and subsequent marches were calm, even if Daley wasn't.

He hid during the rock and egg attack, but he waded into the battle of words, suddenly announcing that the Chicago civil rights movement had been infiltrated by the Communist party. He knew this, he said, because his Police Department's undercover squad had told him. When he was asked to name the "known Communists," he said something about it all being "a matter of record." Soon after he made another startling disclosure: the civil rights movement was being financed in their malicious behavior by the Republican party. Once again, he did not name names. His allegations were bewildering to the city's leading Republicans, who had been such big contributors to his campaign. Now he had them financing the Communists. Before Daley could drag anyone else into his unlikely conspiracy, a fast-moving fire engine snapped him out of his bad-tempered dreamworld and brought him back to reality.

A hook-and-ladder had sped out of its station on the West Side to go to a fire. It was on its way before anybody realized that one man wasn't aboard. He was taking a shower. His job was to steer the rear part of the engine. Without him, the tiller man, the back end was snaking from side to side. It struck a light pole, which fell on a black woman and killed her.

The accident held great significance for the neighborhood because all of the firemen were white, and it was a black slum neighborhood. Civil rights groups had, in fact, been picketing the firehouse, demanding that black firemen be hired, trained, and assigned to the neighborhood. Daley's old Hamburg Club buddy, the siren-blowing Fire Commissioner Quinn, had ignored them. Having anything but an all white fire station in Chicago was almost impossible, because only five percent of the firemen were black.

The night of the accident, angry crowds formed in the neighborhood, and Daley called Quinn and told him to get the white firemen out of there and to put some black ones in. He did—an all black unit, with a white officer in charge.

The next day the rioting broke out, Chicago's first major outburst. It came only months after Daley told the federal government he didn't need its advice, only days after he told the civil rights groups he wouldn't listen to their complaints about Willis, and only days after he said they were a bunch of Republican-financed Communists. Rioting broke out at about the same time in Watts, and when reports of deaths began coming in from L.A., Daley called Governor Kerner and told him he wanted the national guard. Chicago's riot, however, was not as serious as Los Angeles', in which thirty-one people were killed. Nobody was killed during the four nights of Chicago street fighting. About eighty were injured, and most of the property damage was limited to broken windows and overturned cars. The national guard didn't have to leave their armories.

Afterwards, Daley was more subdued than he had been most of the summer, although he still insisted that the rioting was simply "a question of lawlessness, hoodlumism, hooliganism. I don't think there's any connection with civil rights." But he invited the leaders of various civil rights groups to discuss some of the ghetto problems. They met for two hours, and when they finished, Albert Raby, one of the leaders of the anti-Willis movement, said: "It was a totally fruitless meeting. Apparently the mayor called us in to tell us what a great job he had done in spite of the riots, and the meeting accomplished nothing." Daley had brought out his charts and graphs and insisted that his programs for the Negroes were making great progress.

Some of the civil rights people asked him why he didn't fire Willis and integrate the schools, and he said, "I won't inject politics into school matters."

The meeting ended with both sides as far apart as when they began. One of the black leaders said: "For ten years we've been trying to get them to hire more blacks for the Fire Department, and to integrate that firehouse, and we got nowhere. But when somebody gets killed, they manage to find black firemen in one day."

Daley may have truly believed he was doing a fine job for blacks. "Listen," he told an interviewer, "when they had those riots in Harlem, the highest ranking [black] police officer in the city of New York was a lieutenant. We have three Negro commanders. We have seven Negro police captains. In the Fire Department we have two Negro deputy marshals, three battalion chiefs. We have a Negro vehicle commissioner. We have more Negro judges than New York."

Then he'd rattle off the vast sums he had obtained from Washington for the antipoverty war—more than thirty million dollars in less than two years—and point to the hundreds of poor blacks and whites working in antipoverty offices, a growing Head Start program in the schools, an urban renewal program clearing away acres of slums.

On paper it looked good. But contrary to the spirit of the antipoverty legislation, Chicago's program was dominated by City Hall. Not a penny of federal money could come into Chicago without clearing through Daley. Independent agencies had to submit to the Hall's rule. The slightest hint of militancy was enough to bar a group from being funded.

Urban renewal was the greatest deceit. True, slum property was being cleared. But it wasn't being replaced by housing for those who were dispossessed. The poor were moved into other marginal neighborhoods, and highly profitable upper middle class developments replaced the slums. The most glaring example was the Sandburg Village high-rise development, about twelve blocks north of the Loop. It was supposed to have been moderate-income housing. It became one of the most popular places for young, well-off moderns to live, if they could afford the $200-plus rents. On the West Side, where conditions were the worst, nothing was being built, although large tracts of land were available.

Daley complained that the civil rights groups didn't understand what he was doing. They understood: he was maintaining black dependency—always a tenant, never an owner, not quite a citizen.

But they weren't sure what to do about it. The sit-ins and picketing, which had been so effective in the South, didn't have the same impact in Chicago. Even when they sat down in the middle of State Street, jamming Loop traffic, the police calmly placed them in paddy wagons. Unlike the red-necked sheriffs of Alabama, Chicago's police were under strict orders from Superintendent Wilson to use the light touch, especially when the TV cameras were on.

This, ironically, infuriated Daley. He was angrier at Superintendent Wilson than at the marchers. When the traffic blocking began, he wanted the police to get rough, to make mass arrests and to hell with black feelings. Yet, Wilson was the one man in his administration whom he could not order about. He was stuck with Wilson and his independence because Wilson had grown into a civic institution and had remained independent of City Hall. On summer days when small civil rights groups would crisscross downtown, cutting off traffic and angering the downtown crowds, Daley would sit in his office pounding on his desk, waving his arms and cursing Wilson's name.

"It was the most frustrating thing for him," a ward leader said. "He'd sit there blowing his stack and shouting that Wilson was a dumb sonofabitch because he wasn't doing anything about the marchers. God, how he would have loved to see Wilson take a job on the other side of the world. He couldn't wait until Wilson left and he could put somebody in there who'd take orders."

The civil rights groups were kept off balance by Daley's frequent changes in attitude. One day he would be statesmanlike, talking of change in progressive terms. Then he'd become vitriolic and resume his attacks on "outsiders" and "subversive" influences. "He is a difficult man to case," said Rev. Arthur Brazier, the leader of the South Side's Woodlawn Organization, "one of the shrewdest men I've ever had contact with. He could be so disarming and so friendly that the unsophisticated would walk out thinking he had promised them the world, and they wouldn't have had one solid promise. Whenever problems came up and he wanted the help of petty black ministers, he'd send them telegrams inviting them to his office. They'd save those telegrams for years like they were something precious, and take them out of their wallets and show them to people to show they had been there. But just as easily as he could be charming, he could be tough. I remember once when we wanted to establish a community board to pass on urban renewal projects in our area, we told him the Woodlawn Organization wanted to name the members of the board. He absolutely refused. He told us: 'I would never permit the executive office of this city to be co-opted.' So we compromised and agreed to submit a list of names to him, so he chose the board members from the list. That was okay with him. Actually, the results were the same for us, but he got to do it. His powers remained intact."

This was the confusing man Dr. Martin Luther King decided to take on in 1966, when he moved his Southern

Christian Leadership movement north, with Chicago his first target. "King decided to come to Chicago," Brazier said, "because he thought Chicago was unique in that there was one man, one source of power, who you had to deal with. He knew this wasn't the case in New York or any other city. He thought if Daley could be persuaded of the rightness of open housing and integrated schools that things would be done."

Berry, of the Urban League, one of those who briefed King on what to expect from Daley, said, "King thought Daley was a despot and that he ruled with an iron hand, regarding black neighborhoods as plantations to which he anointed his people as overseers. But King also thought that Daley was better than the people around him, and that Daley could be effective if he was convinced of the rightness of King's goals."

And what did Daley think of King?

Outwardly, he treated King with the respect due a world-renowned figure, a Nobel Peace Prize recipient.

But a party leader recalled dropping in on Daley in early 1966, when King was establishing his movement in Chicago. Daley had made a luncheon speech that afternoon, indirectly attacking King.

"Daley asked me what I thought of his speech. I told him: 'Was it necessary to challenge King? Why throw down the gauntlet?'

"He went into a wild rage about King. Oh, the things he said. He called him a dirty sonofabitch, a bastard, a prick. He said: 'King came here to hurt Douglas [Sen. Paul Douglas] because Rockefeller gave him dough, that's why he came here, to try to get Douglas beaten. He's a rabble-rouser, a trouble-maker.'"

Their first meeting, in March 1966, was a bust for King. Daley invited several dozen religious, civil rights, and business leaders to meet with him and his cabinet. King came, but he irritated Daley by bringing along Al Raby, a gaunt schoolteacher who hadn't been invited. Raby was one of the more outspoken new black leaders, and Daley didn't like him.

Then, after the city officials unfurled their charts and talked about their programs, King said Raby would talk for him. Daley frowned and one of his friends among the clergymen cut Raby off to insist that King speak for himself, which King did, warning Daley to expect civil disobedience, talking of the "collective guilt" of all whites for the problems of the Negroes in Chicago, and citing the grievances of blacks. It was nothing Daley hadn't heard before, so his answers were nothing King hadn't heard before: an outline of his programs, a general commitment to solving the problems.

If anything, Daley came out of the meeting with the advantage. King wanted to persuade him of the rightness of King's goals? Fine, he was persuaded, and he was doing everything possible to achieve the goals. Now what? That was King's problem.

It was a problem. King's southern tactics—the peaceful march, the soul-stirring speech—could blow the minds of southern white rustics, but they were old stuff to Chicagoans. Even Daley's Bridgeport neighbors had become accustomed to Gregory's marches. The city's attitude was: let King march around the Loop; we don't live in the Loop. Let him make his speeches and we'll switch TV channels. The city's civic leaders were gracious and outwardly sympathetic. Superintendent Wilson was friendly and accommodating. Before summer even arrived, the movement lost its favorite target: School Superintendent Willis finally resigned and was replaced by an educator with a progressive record and a flair for racial public relations.

King tried moving into a slum to dramatize the housing crisis, but Chicagoans already knew about the slums. Whites were indifferent and Negroes didn't have to be reminded where they lived. Daley even blunted that tactic by unleashing a horde of building inspectors who, for once, wrote up slum violations without holding out their hands for gifts.

Daley was almost smug as he watched King floundering. Then, surprisingly, someone else wiped the smile off his face. Another minority group, the Puerto Ricans, were suddenly heard from when they threw their little ghetto up for grabs.

The Puerto Ricans had settled on the near Northwest Side, along Division Street, moving in when the Poles moved out. The Poles and other slavs had replaced the

Jews, who had come in after the Scandinavians. By the time the Puerto Ricans got there, the neighborhood was well worn.

Except for their music, the Puerto Ricans had been quiet and unobtrusive. Unless one drove through their neighborhood, there was no evidence that they were part of Chicago. Their neighborhood stretched into two wards, but neither of the two aldermen was Puerto Rican. In fact, there wasn't even one Puerto Rican precinct captain.

City Hall didn't bother to extend the usual ethnic courtesies to the Puerto Ricans. When they held their big festival in a local park, Daley and one of their aldermen didn't attend. The other alderman's contribution was a stern warning to the festival organizers not to invite civil rights speakers.

Because they were undemanding and docile, they were cuffed around regularly by the police. The traffic policemen used the Puerto Rican neighborhood to dump their quota of tickets. Few of the policemen assigned to the district spoke Spanish. The Police Department didn't hire many Puerto Ricans because of the minimum height requirements.

One night in June, they blew up. An incident with a couple of heavy-handed cops touched it off, and the riot was on. It was a strange riot. Sometimes the Puerto Ricans didn't appear to be sure if they were having a riot or a festival. But the police treated it as one hundred percent riot, so when it ended after a couple of nights, one youth was dead, a few dozen more were injured, and most of the stores along Division Street were without windows.

The causes were obvious: the usual job and housing discrimination, coupled with the city's indifference and the police's habitual harshness. But Daley promptly blamed the trouble on "outsiders." He hadn't learned a thing from it. And a month later, he and King resumed talking past each other.

They had another meeting, the day after King led a giant Sunday rally and parade in the Loop, tacking a list of demands on the locked door of City Hall. Once again King told him that the housing market in the city had to be opened to blacks. Once again Daley produced a program that he said was in progress. King talked about jobs, and Daley produced another program. This went on for two hours.

Daley came out of the meeting shaking his head and saying, "They have no programs." What he meant was, they had no program that didn't include blacks moving into white neighborhoods.

Two days later, in hundred-degree temperatures, city workers began going through the West Side turning off fire hydrants that the residents had turned on for the kids to play in. For generations, fire hydrants had been turned on in the city's crowded neighborhoods to combat the humid heat of Chicago. Anybody who grew up in Chicago remembers playing in the gush of water. But Fire Chief Quinn had ordered them sealed on the West Side because he didn't want the city's water pressure to drop. Fighting broke out between some of the black residents and the police who were protecting the city crews. It spread, and the riot was on.

It was a big one. For the first time, snipers appeared, firing from the roofs and windows of the public housing projects. Two blacks, one a fourteen-year-old girl, were killed, and dozens more were injured. Five policemen were hurt. Looting spread over several square miles. On the second day, Wilson said the police couldn't handle it and the national guard was called in. On the third morning, Daley appeared on television and said:

"I think you can't charge it directly to Dr. Martin Luther King, but surely some of the people who came in here and have been talking for the last year of violence—they are on his staff. They are responsible in great measure for the instruction that has been given, for the training of these youngsters."

King's people, he seemed to be saying, were behind the hundreds of blacks who were smashing in the windows of white-owned stores that had been overcharging them for years, who were shooting at the police who had been bullying them for years.

Once again he had his "outsiders" to blame for the sores that for many years had been festering without treatment in his city.

But that afternoon he made a quick reverse when he

sat down in his office with King, and other black leaders. The Urban League's Berry was there:

"On the Friday morning after the hydrant riots started we got together in an office downtown to see if we could get some fast action. Ray Simon from the mayor's office was with us, but he said he was there as an observer only. I told him that we wanted to see the mayor, that day, now, and I asked him to arrange it. He said he'd go to City Hall and see about it. I told him: 'There's a phone there, why don't you call?' He wouldn't do it, so we waited. Finally Simon called back and said he couldn't reach the mayor. So I called Daley's secretary and she said she didn't know where he was, so I said: 'We're coming over.' That was about three or four o'clock in the afternoon. When we got there, Daley came in.

"Now that morning, he had that press conference and he implied that Martin caused the riots, that Martin and some of his people had created the atmosphere for them. But in the afternoon, there were no newsmen or cameras in the meeting. It was private, in his office. So he seats Martin next to his desk, where he always puts the leaders of the groups he's seeing, and he says: 'Dr. King, I want to make one thing clear. We know you did nothing to cause the disorders and that you are a man of peace and love.'

"See? It was just the opposite of the statement he made that morning.

"He asked us what we thought could be done. We were worried about now, right now, so we didn't go back to the big problems. We told him to turn on the hydrants, put spray nozzles on them, and start giving black people safe passage to pools in white neighborhoods."

Now there was a program, and Daley liked it. Give them water. He had a whole lake right outside the door. Even before the riots ended a few days later, City Hall had embarked on a crusade to make Chicago's blacks the wettest in the country. Portable swimming pools were being trucked in. Sprinklers were attached to hundreds of hydrants, and water was gushing everywhere. The city's department of planning mobilized to launch a long-range program of black wetness. The Chicago Park District joined in. So did the Fire Department. Suddenly the entire city administration was thinking wet. One cynical civil rights worker said, "I think they're hoping we'll all grow gills and swim away."

Since the pools were an emergency measure, the city didn't have to bother with competitive bidding. So Daley's old Hamburg Club buddy, Fire Chief Quinn, brought a pool-builder friend down from Lake Geneva, Wisconsin, a popular weekend retreat, and cut him in on some of Chicago's pool business. Quinn's friend had built the pool on Quinn's Wisconsin farm.

When Daley emerged from that meeting with King he was finally able to announce that they had reached an agreement. He proudly outlined the wetness program and the headlines chorused: "Peace Plan! Daley-King Agreement Stirs Hope."

Unfortunately for Daley, the black man does not live by water alone. In a month King was marching again, and this time he had Daley worried and in a politically dangerous bind.

King announced that he was going to lead peaceful nondisruptive marches into the city's white neighborhoods, the bungalow and blue-collar belt, to dramatize his plea for open housing. King had finally found the city's soft underbelly, and Daley knew it.

White Chicago could ignore the downtown marches. The riots didn't touch them directly either, since the blacks wrecked their own neighborhood. But white Chicago would react when the hated blacks and liberal white preachers and nuns showed up. Daley knew how they would react, too. It could be 1919 over again. The city's racism, which he insisted wasn't there, would show itself. Daley knew that because if he didn't understand black Chicago, he knew the way white Chicago thought. He knew Bridgeport and that told him about every other neighborhood.

This time he was trapped. He couldn't arrest the marchers as he had done in Bridgeport, because this time they would be led by King, not by Gregory and some unknowns. If he arrested King for trying to lead a peaceful march, he'd be doing something even George Wallace hadn't done on the trek from Selma to Montgomery. He had to protect King and the marchers. To do that, there were bound to be some white heads split, which would be shown in living color on TV, and seen by the millions of white voters. And the fall elections were only ten weeks off. King had him.

The first march went into Gage Park, on the far Southwest Side. Many of the people in Gage Park had formerly lived in Englewood, Woodlawn, and other areas that had slowly turned black. They were Lithuanian, Polish, Italian in ancestry. They were blue collar in occupation, and they were haters. It was an ugly event. King was hit in the head with a rock. The bump was headlined around the world.

Daley pleaded publicly for King to come back to the conference table, to call off the marches. "There must be some way of resolving questions without marches," he said, looking plaintively into the camera.

Two days later, on a beautiful Sunday afternoon, the marchers went into Cragin, another bungalow section on the far Northwest Side. King had been taken ill, but the other civil rights leaders were there, along with a large turnout of priests and nuns. Cragin is a heavily Catholic area, with many Poles and Italians, but that didn't keep the nuns and priests from getting a face full of spit.

Once again it was nasty. The police kept the marchers on one side of the street, and the hecklers on the other, but many of the whites tried to break through. Others went in alleys behind the buildings and lofted rocks and bottles over the roofs. Their hearts weren't in it, but the police waded in, and that night the sight and sounds of clubs against a couple of white skulls, and white voices crying "brutality," poured out of the TV sets.

King's people said that was just the beginning. They were going to hold not one, but two, maybe three, marches a day, in different parts of town. Then they were going to march into the hard-nosed suburb of Cicero. When a Cicero politician heard their plan, he said simply, "Jesus, they won't make it. If they get in, they won't get out alive."

The white neighborhoods were furious, and much of their anger was directed at Daley. He had given the rioting blacks swimming pools, now the police were beating home-owning whites. The city's establishment was joining in, expressing disapproval of the new tactic. Even Archbishop Cody, who had earlier supported King's goals and demands, paying the price with sharply reduced Sunday collections in the backlash neighborhoods, now joined the chorus of those asking King to desist and get himself back to the good old conference table. James Bevel, one of King's men, snapped back: "When there's trouble, Daley sticks up his liberal bishop to say, 'You've gone far enough.' Well, we've got news for the man. If the archbishop doesn't have the courage to speak up for Christ, let him join the devil."

King had Daley reeling. If the marches increased in number the police couldn't possibly protect all the marchers. Blacks would be hurt, and the black neighborhoods might retaliate. Another 1919 was getting closer all the time, and the Hamburg Club was getting too old for that sort of thing.

Daley sent his legal department into court for an emergency injunction limiting the number of marches to one a day, requiring advance notice, and setting other ground rules. That cut off the immediate crisis, and if the blacks violated the court order the police could arrest them, which would look good on TV.

Then he called for a "summit conference," a mighty meeting of the city's business, religious, political, and civil rights leaders, to hammer out once and for all an agreement on housing, education, jobs, and the other weighty problems. Actually, all that was needed was for his administration to do its job, but with a "summit conference" there was always a chance he could talk his way out of it.

The conference, held in a Protestant church, found Daley and his group on the defensive. The civil rights groups laid out their demands—the same ones they had been making all summer. This time, however, Daley began giving ground, making concessions. He was calm, placating, even when the militants were sharp and argumentative. "At one point," Berry said, "Tom Keane leaned over and stage-whispered to Daley: 'Fuck 'em, Dick, we don't have to stay here and listen to this.' But Daley was friendly and controlled."

Daley got what he needed—a brief delay. A subcommittee was formed to work out the specifics of the "summit agreement." Between the injunction against mass marches and the subcommittee, Daley had time to breathe. Eight days later, the agreement was drafted and both sides met again at the summit and signed their names. There was great rejoicing.

King: "It is the first step in a thousand-mile journey, but an important step . . . one of the most significant programs ever conceived to make open housing a reality. . . . Never before have such far-reaching and creative concepts been made."

Daley: "I'm satisfied that the people of Chicago and the suburbs and the whole metropolitan area will accept this program in the light of the people who endorsed it. This program was worked out by the people of the Chicago Freedom Movement, labor unions, business groups and civic groups."

It was an impressive document, chock full of noble vows and promises. It was also without legal standing and wasn't worth the paper it was printed on. Only three months after it was signed, when the crisis was over, Alderman Keane said at a City Council meeting that "There is no Summit Agreement," and the people who took part in the meeting had merely agreed that open housing was "a goal to be reached," but there was no agreement beyond that.

He could say it then. The snow had fallen, Dr. King was back home in the South, the marches had faded into memory. Daley hadn't rejected Keane's suggestion to "fuck 'em." He just did it slowly.

Chapter VIII

> KUNSTLER: Mayor Daley, in one of your answers to my questions, you stated something about your instructions to offer hospitality to people coming to Chicago. In view of what you said, did you consider the use of night sticks on the heads of demonstrators hospitable?
>
> FORAN: Objection, your honor.
>
> HOFFMAN: I sustain the objection.

Under the election laws, Daley couldn't start his fourth term without standing for reelection, so when 1967 drew near, the Republicans began looking for a volunteer to stand in the path of the Machine.

Most Republicans tried not to think about it, but several felt they should do more than go through the motions. The party had risen from the grave in the November 1966 county and state elections and had cut into Daley's kingdom. For the second time Daley had misjudged the voter appeal of a seemingly bland, stolid, young lawyer named Richard Ogilvie. The first time, in 1962, Daley ran a political amateur for sheriff and Ogilvie beat him. He did a reform job on the sheriff's office and ran for president of the County Board. Again, Daley underestimated Ogilvie and put up a loud-talking party hack. Ogilvie won again, as did Republican candidates for sheriff and county treasurer, and industrialist Charles Percy, who unseated the venerable Sen. Paul Douglas.

With the momentum of those victories, and the hundreds of patronage jobs Ogilvie picked up for the party, some Republicans wanted to give Daley a fight. Even in losing, they argued, the party could be strengthened in the city.

One of them was John Waner, an energetic, self-made liberal Republican businessman who had been Percy's Chicago campaign manager.

"I went to Ogilvie and Percy and told them that I thought we had a good chance to make Daley work for it, providing we came up with a substantial candidate, someone like Lindsay, who could face the issues of the day. I told them we couldn't go with another Sheehan or Adamowski, or any of the nobodies. They agreed and said they'd try to find somebody. The trouble is that everybody they talked to didn't want it. They knew they wouldn't get the support of the papers or the business community, so they figured, why bother? Another thing was that most of the Republicans who might have filled the bill lived in the suburbs. I went to see Ogilvie again and said: 'What are we going to do? We have to have a candidate.' He said: 'John, it looks like you'll have to take him on yourself.' "

So Waner, a stubby, raspy-voiced, excitable, white-haired man, who had made a small fortune in the heating and air conditioning business, volunteered for the hopeless job.

"I started by getting together with teams of Republican ward committeemen and talking to them about what issues would be the best in their areas. I hate to say it, but most of them told me that unless I really ran a knock-the-nigger-down campaign, I wouldn't have a prayer. I couldn't do that. It was against my grain and I told them so.

"So I went after the real issues. I hit hard at the inadequacies in housing in the city. I'd been federal housing director in Chicago when Eisenhower was in, so I knew what the problems were. Then I went into the problems of Negroes being kept out of the trade unions. That was two years before it became a big civil rights issue. I laid out how the unions were discriminating against blacks and that the city was doing nothing to combat it.

"What did it get me? I'd draw up a big position paper, make a speech, then I'd look in the newspapers and I'd be somewhere in the back pages. The papers seemed to be more interested in trying to find out if I had a criminal record. Somebody in City Hall had dug around and found out that I had been in a little trouble when I was just a kid. It was just neighborhood punk stuff and it hadn't amounted to anything. Here I am talking about the issues, and I'm being asked if I have ever been in prison. At least we cleared that up.

"Money. I figured I'd need a minimum of half a million to run a decent campaign. I wound up spending $100,000 and I had to hit my own bank account for some of that. One of the big State Street storeowners promised me a campaign contribution one day, then he took a long vacation starting the next day.

"I got together in my house one morning to talk about black problems with Dick Gregory. I didn't publicize it because I just wanted the benefit of his thinking. Then some columnist writes that I'm cooking ham and eggs for Gregory, which wasn't true because Gregory is a vegetarian and wouldn't eat ham, and then the Democratic precinct captains had thousands of copies run off and they circulated them in the white backlash neighborhoods.

"No matter what I said, regardless of the issue, the papers treated me as if I didn't exist. The *Tribune* actually put me back on the obituary page one day, and they're supposed to be a Republican paper. I was really hurting for something big that would let people know I was there."

Waner got lucky. Something big did come along when his campaign was at its flattest. One morning the city's convention hall—one of the biggest and newest in the world—burned to the ground. Built only a few years earlier at a cost of $35,000,000, it had been one of the great ribbon-cutting triumphs of Daley's administration. It was also a cause of anger for the city's conservationists and architects. A battle had been waged by the conservationists to keep it from being built on the lake front, where it would gobble up hundreds of acres of precious park land. The conservationists rightly argued that the lake front had to be preserved for the city's millions of people and that the visiting conventioneers were more interested in bars and women than scenery. But the powerful *Chicago Tribune* was determined, for inexplicable reasons, to see it built along the lake and named after the late Col. Robert McCormick, their publisher. They pushed so hard in Springfield for the enabling legislation that one angry legislator demanded on the floor that the *Tribune*'s political editor be required to register as a lobbyist. Between the *Tribune* and Daley, the conservationists were beaten and it was built. Architects and most people with two eyes hailed it as one of the ugliest big buildings ever seen—a shapeless mass of concrete, squatting like a gray sow along the blue waters of Lake Michigan.

When it burned, Waner had his bread-and-butter issue. Old frame buildings burn to the ground, but not big, new modern buildings. What kind of construction was it? Were the taxpayers' millions squandered on cheap shortcuts? Was the fireproofing made of tissue paper? What happened, Dick Daley? The headlines danced before Waner's eyes.

"The morning it burned I went to my campaign headquarters and the information was already coming in. Firemen were tipping me off on the inadequate hydrant system out there. I was getting calls from engineers. Somebody else told me a politician held the insurance on the place. So I issued a statement in the morning calling for an investigation. Then I told my people to get going on the research. I had just said it when George Tagge, the *Tribune*'s political editor, rushed in and said I should shut up about McCormick Place, that didn't I know he built it, that in Springfield when they were pushing it through they even called it Tagge's Temple? He said that if I started blasting away at it, it might embarrass him and the *Tribune,* so I had to shut up. I said the *Tribune* wasn't doing anything for me anyway. So Tagge said, yeah, but at least they weren't hurting me. So I gave up. The *Trib* runs the Republican party in this state, so what could I do? I shut up about the fire. I figured to hell with it. After that, the only time I made a big headline during the whole campaign was when I said that if I was elected I'd fire Orlando Wilson. When I said that, they made it the number one headline. When I talked about important issues, they ignored me. When I said I'd fire one guy, it got me the biggest headline of the day. It was very frustrating."

Daley could have gone fishing and come back after the election to be sworn in. His Non-Partisan Committee to Reelect Daley had grown until it was almost a Chicago who's who, although half of the people in it lived in the suburbs, some outside of Cook County or in other states. The rest of them lived in the luxury high-rise belt, but the hundreds of prominent names looked impressive in the full-page newspaper ads they took. All four papers, including the Republican *Tribune,* endorsed him. The Machine was operating efficiently; yet Daley campaigned surprisingly hard. He was angered by the recent loss of county offices and the defeat of Douglas, and he wanted to reassert the Machine's city strength. There was also a matter to settle with King and the other militant blacks who had plagued him so the summer before. At one of their meetings, King had reminded him that the black vote put him across in 1963 and that it might be needed for the same purpose in 1967. "Our vote will be the balance of power," King said. Daley had coolly answered, "All the people of the community will elect the mayor." He wanted to show King what he meant.

He won bigger than ever before: seventy-three percent of the vote, a plurality of 519,696 votes, and he carried all fifty wards. Waner didn't even carry his home ward, in which he had long been the Republican committeeman. It was a humiliating defeat. Even Daley felt sorry for Waner.

"It's funny about losing. People stay away from you. The night I lost, I didn't get any phone calls. And the next morning I was at my office and by 10:30 nobody called to say they were sorry. Boy, do you feel alone when you get clobbered. Then my phone rang. It was Daley. He said something like: 'John, this is Mayor Daley. I'm not calling to gloat. You ran a decent campaign, John, and I know how it feels to lose. I lost when I ran for sheriff in 1946.' It was nice of him to call. You know, I had forgotten that he had ever lost an election until he told me."

The overwhelming victory, with both black and white majorities, was only part of his response to King's political impertinence. The rest came in his inauguration speech when he made his most significant pledge for the coming four years: "As long as I am mayor, law and order will prevail."

It was more than mere phrase-making. He was shedding the uncomfortable pose of the sometime liberal and was becoming his real self at last—the tough-talking authoritarian who wasn't going to let anybody push him around or get out of line. There would be no more of the "Dr. King, I know you are a man of love and peace" approach to those who threatened him. By early summer Daley was ranting: "He [King] is a trouble maker. He doesn't know our problems. He lives in Atlanta. We don't need him to tell us what to do. He only comes here for one purpose, or to any other city he has visited, and that is to cause trouble." They were virtually the same words that had been spoken by the white establishment in Selma, Montgomery, and other southern cities, while northern leaders such as Daley clucked over the South's rigidity and ruthlessness.

When riots broke out in Detroit and Newark he immediately announced that he was alerting the national guard here because he had reason to believe a national plot to riot existed and Chicago was one of the targets in the conspiracy. He appeared on television and blustered: "I can assure you there won't be any blank ammunition [in the national guard rifles]. The ammunition will be live."

The tough approach wasn't limited to words. Orlando Wilson had retired shortly after the reelection, and Daley could now pick up the phone and issue an order that would be obeyed by the police chief. Wilson's retirement and return to California had been a complete surprise. He had repeatedly said that he would serve "as long as the mayor wants me." He had become as well known in Chicago as Daley himself, was highly respected, and had become part of the city's civic establishment. In seven years he had made visible changes in the Police Department, making it probably the most technically modern unit in the world and eliminating most of the blatant corruption and graft. A strict disciplinarian, he had curbed the natural instinct of Chicago policemen to knock around the poor, the black, and the politically impotent. When he retired, several civil rights leaders expressed regret. They had reason to. Out on the street, the police sensed what Daley wanted and began pushing blacks harder.

Wilson said he retired because he was sixty-seven and wanted to relax. But for a long time rumors persisted that he had been deftly eased out by Daley, who wanted someone who would follow his get-tough orders. In Wilson's replacement, James Conlisk, Daley had such a man. Conlisk's father had been a friend of Daley's, and was one of the seven aged, politically heavy, assistant superintendents who ran the Police Department in the pre-Wilson days. The younger Conlisk, while an able administrator, had none of Wilson's personal stature and independence. He would say "yes sir" when Daley told him what to do.

Whether by threats, bluff, luck, the general sagging of the civil rights movement, the distraction of antiwar protest, or the tendency of blacks to withdraw and reject the concept of integration, Daley got through the summer of 1967 without any major incidents. It could have even been Chicago's wet-the-black program, which took on the proportions of Niagara Falls. As Daley said in one speech: "Private and public agencies are operating 133 swimming pools and for the first time this year 55 of these pools have opened for weekend and evening swimming . . . more than 200 spray pools are in operation and the Fire Department is offering splash parties for youngsters at 80 local schools." There shouldn't have been a dry black in Chicago.

Once again, Daley was being praised as something of a municipal marvel, the one man who could keep his city cool during the hottest of the hot summers. Once again he was the man, the magazines said, who had the answers, the programs, who knew how to get things done, who, almost alone among city leaders, was making progress.

And on the West Side, when the summer ended, a young

black man stood on the screened-in balcony that encircled the entire thirteenth floor of the housing project he lived in, serving as an outdoor hallway and playground for his four children and the hundreds of others who lived in the building, and he talked about the way he saw progress.

"I look around me, I feel like this is a foreign country. I don't belong. My boss is a Jew, he lives in the suburbs. My foreman is a Pole. They think colored people don't know much. I take home ninety-one dollars a week, and I'm never gonna be the foreman. No brother ever gonna be the foreman where I work.

"See down there? See that pool, that little bathtub? They put that there after the riots. How many kids could get in that pool? Fifty maybe? Well we got five hundred kids, maybe more than that, all playing out on these balconies.

"See this balcony, these outside hallways? That's my kids' playground. And when that wire fence tears through those little babies fall through and die. Man, this is real isolation. Even the police are afraid to come in here.

"Last week a white bus driver threw this old colored winehead off the bus on the corner out there—threw him off. I ran with some brothers and we beat the driver with bats. Two CTA detectives come and we beat them. When the police came we ran back in here and the police were afraid to come in here after us.

"Last year there was all that trouble, the police were clearing everybody off the streets, and these little boys, they were playing, they didn't know any better, and the police took those little boys and threw them down into a pile on the sidewalk. They just threw those little boys in a pile. Then they started loading them into a wagon. I came down and I said, 'You got my little brother in there.' They said, 'Get out, nigger, or you'll be in there, too.' I came back up here and I got my gun and I started shooting. I don't know if I hit anybody, but I was trying. I feel like this—if I got killed up here, I wouldn't be in the wrong. Cat can be walking down the street minding his own business and a cop grabs him, shakes him, throws him in the car. Twelve of my friends got arrested last week just that way. My brothers been pushed around too long. Well, I get zapped walking down the street, I'm not going to cop out. I'd go right out there and shoot."

If the angry young black man was standing on his balcony a few months later, and if the smoke wasn't too thick, he might have seen a helicopter circling slowly over the West Side, over the burning buildings, the dead black bodies in the alleys.

The nun had once asked him please, Mr. Mayor, come out there and see how the people are suffering. And he had said, Sister, the bootstraps, let them pull harder. Now he had finally gone out to the West Side, in a helicopter, to see what people do when they have no boots.

King had died on Thursday, April 4, and everybody knew, or should have known, what was going to happen. The Police Department knew and canceled all leaves and days off. They concentrated their strength in the Loop to protect the stores and businesses should the blacks come downtown for revenge.

The South Side was strangely peaceful. There, in the older ghetto, life wasn't quite as hopeless. Workers had gone out from the Woodlawn Organization, the influential grassroots alliance run by the Reverend Brazier, and were maintaining calm. The few black independent aldermen were moving around, helping cool it. Even the tough, black street gangs—also well organized—were discouraging riots. Why burn what we have, was the attitude. The South Side had leaders and the leaders were black.

It blew on the West Side, and when Daley climbed in the helicopter with Fire Chief Quinn, scores of buildings were burning, several people had already been killed by police, dozens were wounded, and it was a devastated, looted, bleeding place.

The helicopter flew over the Twenty-ninth Ward, a cesspool of black slums. The ward boss of the Twenty-ninth was Bernie Neistein, a Mafia front man who was white and rich and lived in a lake front high-rise. The black alderman took orders from Neistein. Then it flew over the black Twenty-fourth Ward. In the Twenty-fourth, the black alderman took orders from Carmen Fratto and Irwin Horwitz, both white. Horwitz, a rich real estate man, was a big money raiser for the Machine and always had a city job with a fine title. All the precinct captains in the Twenty-fourth were white, although the ward had been black for years. Horwitz said the blacks couldn't handle the job. Then it flew over the Twenty-seventh Ward, which is just about all black. The boss of the Twenty-seventh was Ed Quigley, who was white. Quigley made $28,000 a year running the city sewer system. Quigley's alderman was also white. Then it flew over the mostly black Twenty-eighth Ward, which was bossed by Tony Girolami, who was white, and had an alderman named Joe Jambrone, who was white. It also flew over the black neighborhoods that stuck into the edges of the First Ward, which was run by John D'Arco, who was white, and into the Twenty-fifth, which was run by Vito Marzullo who was white, and into the Twenty-sixth, which was run by Matthew Bieszczat, who was white. It flew over the black legislative districts that were represented in Springfield by Larry DiPrima and Louie Capuzi, by John Touhy and Pete Granata, by Vic Arrigo and Matt Ropa, by Larry Bartels and Bernie McDevitt, by Bob McPartlin and Frank Wolfe, by Bernie Neistein, Sam Romano and Zygmunt Sokolnicki, all of whom were white.

Daley got off the helicopter and said, "I never believed that it would happen here."

Quinn goaded him during the flight, pointing out looters below, urging that they be shot on sight, that anybody starting a fire be shot. His firemen were in danger, he said, especially his white firemen, since he had few of the other kind. Quinn pleaded that Daley crack down harder, that the police open up. Quinn, the man who turned on air raid sirens to celebrate baseball victories, the man who sent firemen jogging on expressways, the man who had been caught using firemen to work on his weekend farm, was now making life-death judgments.

Daley called Conlisk in and demanded to know why police had not been ordered to shoot arsonists and looters.

"Mr. Mayor, you issued no such orders," Conlisk said.

Daley snapped, "You are the superintendent of police."

Daley later called a press conference and, in cold anger and a flat, hard voice, said:

"I have conferred with the superintendent of police this morning and I gave him the following instructions: I said to him very emphatically and very definitely that an order be issued by him immediately and under his signature to shoot to kill any arsonist or anyone with a molotov cocktail in his hand because they're potential murderers, and to issue a police order to shoot to maim or cripple anyone looting any stores in our city. Above all, the crime of arson is to me the most hideous and worst crime of any and should be dealt with in this fashion.

"I was most disappointed to know that every policeman out on his beat was supposed to use his own discretion and this decision was his [Conlisk's]. In my opinion, policemen should have had instructions to shoot arsonists and looters —arsonists to kill and looters to maim and detain.

"I assumed the instructions were given, but the instructions to the police were to use their own judgment. I assumed any superintendent would issue instructions to shoot arsonists on sight and to maim the looters, but I found out this morning that this wasn't so, and therefore gave him specific instructions."

"What about children," somebody asked.

"You wouldn't want to shoot them," Daley said, "but with Mace you could detain youngsters."

The order became the most famous utterance of his career. He was promptly assailed by prominent liberals, blacks, moderates, churchmen, and just about everybody to the left of Barry Goldwater. How can a policeman be sure he will merely wound a looter, the critics asked; are they such fine shots that they can avoid hitting an artery in the leg, or aiming a bit higher and getting somebody in the spine for running away with a lamp? Can they know that the man with a threatening-looking bottle in his hand isn't carrying a bomb, but merely some booze?

Two days later, when the riots were ending, Daley said he had been misunderstood and modified his statement, scurrying back to the generally accepted principle of "minimum force." His press aide, Earl Bush, blamed the misunderstanding on the press. "It was damn bad reporting," he said. "They should have printed what he meant, not what he said." This approach to journalism would have been difficult in covering Daley, since he is given to saying things like: "Today the real problem is the future." Once, while discussing antiwar dissent, he said, "I don't see any more serious division in our country than we had in the Civil War and at other times." And while telling a neighborhood rally about plans he had for their community, he said, "We want to make Austin in the future what it has always been in the past." Printing what he meant, and not what he said, might have been journalism's greatest challenge.

Not that he was really concerned with the horrified reaction of the less bloodthirsty. His director of special events was put in charge of tabulating the public's reaction to his shoot-to-kill order, and a week later he triumphantly announced that ten thousand letters and one thousand telegrams had been received by City Hall, and they were running fifteen to one in favor of shooting to kill. If the American Civil Liberties Union didn't approve, the white people in Gage Park and Cragin did, and they had many more votes than the ACLU.

Daley appointed the usual commission of prominent citizens and experts to investigate the riot. It later agreed with the Kerner report that the frustrations of ghetto life was the cause, not a "conspiracy," as Daley had charged. It also urged that the earlier recommendations of the Kerner report be followed, but by that time a survey of aldermen had showed that a majority of them had not read the Kerner report and didn't intend to.

The commission recommended that Daley's Police Department stop applying one standard of treatment to blacks and another to whites.

This recommendation was followed. The police didn't stop mistreating blacks, but they did begin treating whites just as brutally. It was equality of sorts.

Chapter IX

KUNSTLER: Mayor Daley, on the twenty-eighth of August, 1968, did you say to Senator Ribicoff . . .

FORAN: Oh, your honor, I object.

KUNSTLER: ". . . fuck you, you Jew son of a bitch, you lousy motherfucker, go home?"

FORAN: Listen to that! I object to that kind of conduct in a courtroom. Of all the improper, foolish questions. Typical, Your Honor, of making up questions that have nothing to do with the lawsuit.

HOFFMAN: I sustain the objection.

His mind was made up. The convention was going to be held in Chicago, and not just in Chicago, Illinois, a large midwest, industrial city, located on the shores of Lake Michigan, with ample hotel facilities and public transportation, the jet crossroads of the nation. It was going to be held in a place known as Daley's Chicago. The names in the city's 1,708-page phone book ranged from Harry Aabel to Zeke Zzzypt, with a few million others in between, and a black man named Jean Baptiste Point du Sable became the first settler in 1784, but in August 1968, it was to be Daley's Chicago. As his special events director put it, while coaching some politicians and convention workers at a luncheon, "Remember to impress on the visiting delegates that they are not just visiting Chicago, but Mayor Daley's Chicago."

The man himself was even more specific about where the nation's Democrats would meet, when he said, "I would say that it is an important sign of faith to the American people for this national convention to be held here, not in some resort center, but in the very heart of a great city, where people live and work and raise their families, and in one of the biggest neighborhoods in Chicago—*my* neighborhood!" Not many men could say they brought a national political convention to their own neighborhood.

Other cities wanted it when the choice was being made late in 1967, but few cities had a mayor who, with a hundred or so delegates in his pocket, could go straight to the White House to make his pitch. His arguments were persuasive. He had avoided race riots in 1967, while other cities were burning; he was tough enough to maintain law and order, and he needed the convention to be sure of delivering Illinois' twenty-seven electoral votes to President Johnson in the 1968 election. The war had cut into Johnson's Illinois popularity and 1968 would not be the cakewalk that 1964 was. President Johnson had wanted the convention in Houston, but Daley argued that since he was sure of carrying Texas, why waste the convention on it? At the time these discussions were being held, it was generally accepted that a convention helped a party in the state where it was held. Daley had not yet single-handedly reversed this principal.

Beyond those arguments for Chicago, there were others that were not talked about. The Democrats had not come to Chicago since 1956, when he was new in the mayor's office, and not yet a "king maker." They had not seen the things he had built, the towers, the airport, the expressways: Daley's Chicago. Also, he was the second most powerful Democrat in the nation, so why should somebody else have the glory of being host to his political party, why should somebody else's city be bounced off Telstar to the TV screens of the world?

Johnson decided Daley was right. It would be hard to

say that a man who had delivered his state by 800,000 votes the last time was wrong. But within six months, the guarantee of racial calm had gone up in the West Side's smoke after Dr. King's death, Johnson had announced that he wasn't going to run again, antiwar groups were making plans to come to Chicago to protest our involvement in Vietnam, and Democrats were wishing the convention had been awarded to some place like Nome, Alaska.

Daley, however, insisted that there was nothing to worry about. "As long as I am mayor," he vowed, over and over again, "there will be law and order in Chicago. Nobody is going to take over this city."

Those who wondered what means he would employ to maintain law and order got two examples. First, there was the order to shoot to kill or maim. Then came what was almost a dress rehearsal of the Democratic Convention. Nothing that happened in August should have been a surprise after the events that occurred on a balmy Saturday afternoon in Chicago on April 27, 1968.

Early in the year, the Chicago Peace Council, made up of some two hundred peace groups, made plans to hold an antiwar rally and parade. They wanted to meet in Grant Park, listen to speeches, parade through the Loop, hold a rally at the Civic Center plaza. None of their plans were uncommon. Grant Park is the Loop's green front yard, State Street is the city's parade grounds, and the spacious Civic Center plaza had become the city's most popular gathering place.

To get permits, the organizers had to contact not one, but three separate city agencies, all controlled directly or indirectly by the mayor.

First they went to the Chicago Park District, which stalled, obstructed, and deceived them. One tactic was to demand almost a million dollars in insurance and bonds for the one-day event, although the Park District carries considerable insurance with one of the city's politician-insurance agents. Then the Park District flatly refused to issue them a permit. William McFetridge, the district's president and the mayor's good friend from organized labor, said it was the district's new policy to "keep unpatriotic groups and race agitators from using the parks." One year earlier, a newspaper columnist had picked up the phone and asked the Park District for some space to run a mongrel dog show on a Sunday as a fun event for his readers. The district's general superintendent, without discussing insurance, patriotism, or race, said, "I'll give you more than park land—I'll give you Soldier Field that day," which he did, even providing park employees to walk behind the hundreds of dogs, cleaning up after them. But the peace groups, which could be expected to show better manners than the dogs, could not get permission to use a few acres of land that were just sitting there anyway. Only the threat of a federal law suit moved the Park District to relent and end the weeks of obstruction.

That took care of the starting point for the peace march. Next came the parade itself. For a parade permit they went to the Department of Streets and Sanitation in City Hall, and one of the mayor's cabinet members. They were told that a parade on that date was absolutely out because another group planned a parade earlier in the day and only one parade a day is allowed in Chicago's Loop. After lengthy negotiations, the Department of Streets and Sanitation grudgingly consented that the peace marchers could walk on the sidewalk, as pedestrians, under police control, from Grant Park to the Civic Center plaza. That took care of the parade, modified to a pedestrian walk.

Next came the use of the Civic Center plaza, which is under the control of the Public Building Commission, a governmental agency created for the purpose of putting up public buildings without submitting the projects to the voters under a referendum. Daley is president of the commission, and it is managed by a private real estate firm owned by one of his friends. Although the Civic Center is a public building, built at taxpayers' expense, its plaza is not public. The Public Building Commission has taken the position that it is private property and they can decide who can walk on it. It decided that the peace marchers could not walk on it on April 27. The plaza was being "caulked" by workmen so it would be off limits to the public that day. Actually, the caulking had been going on all week, while thousands of people used the plaza. Several formal gatherings had been held while the caulking was being done by simply roping off the tiny work area.

After further haggling, the Public Building Commission agreed that the peace groups could march to the sidewalks around the half-square-block plaza, stand on the sidewalks a few minutes, then disperse.

With these severe limitations agreed to, the march was held. About six thousand people met in Grant Park. Like most of the people who turn out for large peace rallies, they were predominantly white, all ages, middle and upper middle class. They were orderly, relaxed, and cheerful.

Five hundred policemen in riot helmets were assigned to the march, an extraordinarily large force. No more than one hundred are assigned to Wrigley Field for the forty-five thousand Bear fans, with their pints of brandy. The large police unit was surprising also in the absence of even the mildest hint of trouble. No wild-talking hippies had taken part in the planning. Of the two hundred groups participating, only a few were extreme in their politics.

During the two-mile walk, no windows were broken, nothing was thrown, the police were not taunted. Some of the younger marchers chanted "No more war" and "Hell no, we won't go," but the word "pig" wasn't uttered once. Not even a small "oink." The marchers, strung out for blocks, stayed on the sidewalk. Yet the policemen who walked along the edge of the street held their billy clubs in their hands.

The first marchers reached the plaza and took their places on the plaza's edge behind a thin, easily breakable plastic cord that had been set up as a barrier. Policemen, a few yards apart, positioned themselves inside the plastic cord. Other policemen stood on the curb to keep the crowd from going into the street. The marchers arrived in small groups, delayed by green lights along the way. Some said the police held them at corners for as long as three lights.

Before more than half of the original group from the park had arrived at the plaza, and while room remained on the sidewalk, the police decided that they should begin dispersing.

Nobody knows for certain where it began. Later reports say it may have started when about a dozen people, out of the three thousand who were standing peacefully, snapped the thin plastic line and tried to sit down on the plaza. Another version said that one young man jumped into the waters of the plaza's reflecting pool. All witnesses, including the police, agreed that there were no rocks, eggs, or punches thrown. But within minutes, it was a mini-version of Michigan and Balbo in August.

The policemen within the plaza began warning the crowd to disperse. Some of the people turned to go, only to be met by policemen standing in the gutter, who threatened them if they stepped off the sidewalk into the street. It was a nightmarish pincer, with clubs brandished ahead and behind.

One long-haired young man was suddenly yanked from the crowd, dragged into the plaza by several policemen, and flung into the pool. Then they pulled him from the pool, dragged him across the plaza, and flung him against a wall. Another man refused to lower his peace sign and was pulled from the crowd and beaten. Another was knocked down and, while half conscious and thoroughly subdued, was sprayed in the face with Mace.

Some people got across the street and ran into restaurants, hoping to hide over a sandwich and a cup of coffee. Policemen went in, dragged them out, and beat them. A long-haired man who had left the rally early to browse in a nearby bookstore came out of the store without knowing what was happening. He was struck on the head with a club.

The police began making arrests, finally, and there was little resistance. People were too stunned. But after one paddy wagon was filled, a policeman thrust a can of Mace inside, sprayed the interior then closed the door. Several shoppers and workers who weren't in the rally, but just happened to be walking by, were beaten. Marchers who had cameras were forced to surrender their film. Film was also confiscated at the police station from those arrested.

Once the crowd broke and scattered, the police didn't let up. Moving in teams, policemen chased people for four and five blocks, pummeling their backs and legs and chanting rhythmically, "Move, move, get out of the Loop, move, move, get out of the Loop."

The police showed clearly that Saturday, four months before the convention, that they were capable of staging what the Walker Report later described as a "police riot," and that they could do it without their being subjected to the allegedly intolerable abuse they supposedly endured during the Democratic Convention. That Saturday in Chicago, there were few provocative acts directed at them. They attacked a basically peaceful crowd, before the eyes of the highest-ranking officers on the department, including Superintendent Conlisk himself. After witnessing his police go berserk—the term overreact had not yet been concocted to describe police brutality—Conlisk said his men had acted properly.

The people who were beaten turned to the city's four newspapers that night and the next day, and to the television news shows, for accounts of the brutality, angry editorials, demands for a thorough investigation. They were amazed to find the story almost ignored. The stories were sketchy, often in error, and inconclusive. It might have been nothing more than a brawl in a neighborhood bar. Most of them assumed that the news media had collaborated with the police, but the explanation was less sinister: because peace marches in Chicago had been uneventful in the past, and because no threat of trouble preceded this one, the news media had provided minimal coverage. One paper didn't assign anybody because it does not publish on Sunday. Others sent only one reporter or only a photographer. The television stations were also unprepared. By Monday, when the media's full staffs came to work, the stories were already of the dull, follow-up variety. There was one other factor in the sparse news coverage of so significant an event: a pure and simple police riot had not occurred in Chicago before, at least not in modern times and not to white people in broad daylight. Those who hadn't been there didn't believe it had happened. They assumed it had begun with an assault on police, and they attributed the reports from the victims to the tendency of liberals to magnify police misconduct—the Anne Frank syndrome, as someone once put it, forgetting that there had been a real Anne Frank, and that her story was hardly exaggerated.

Yet it should not have been a complete surprise. Discipline on the Police Department had been eroding since the retirement of Superintendent Wilson. Complaints of brutality, especially from blacks and long-haired youths, had increased sharply. At the same time, cases of punishment of policemen for such acts had declined. The police had returned to their old code of protecting each other. The Internal Investigations Division, a self-policing unit set up by Wilson, had become known as a pail of whitewash. Pressures unique to police work had also intensified with the riots, demonstrations, the rise of black militancy. The people in the April 27 peace march weren't black, but they represented other enemies of police: the liberal, the Left, the young, and the upper middle class.

Chicago policemen, like most policemen, reflect blue-collar values. Most of them live in the city's bungalow belt because they are required by law to live in the city, so they share the community feelings toward the suburban liberal who wants them to integrate, while the suburbs remain white. Many policemen are veterans and in a quasi-military job, so they dislike the peace groups. And the Chicago police had been steeped in simplistic political philosophy. The department's Intelligence Division, known as the Red Squad, is one of the biggest political intelligence units outside of the FBI. Most of its members, however, can't differentiate between a housewife marching for peace and a member of the radical Weathermen. Anything to the left of their neighborhood American Legion is radical-revoluntionary-Red. By 1968 they had taken to raiding innocent fund-raising parties for peace groups under the pretext of minors being served liquor; harassing other groups by constantly photographing people who attend their meetings; feeding vicious misinformation to the pink-baiting *Chicago Tribune* and other right-wing publications, and sharing information with ultra-right oddities, such as the Church League of America. A police department whose membership had, only eight years earlier, been exposed as the most corrupt in the United States, had taken upon itself the role of protecting Chicago from the "Red menace." To the police, the peace marchers were part of the menace.

Daley did nothing about the first police riot, although he was bombarded with complaints from the victims and from people who had seen it, including some from conservatives who, while not sympathetic to the marchers, were appalled by the police attack. By doing nothing, Daley permitted the police to take off both gloves. The first had come off after the shoot-to-kill order.

By midsummer, both sides were girding for action. The Yippies were armed with a vivid imagination to match their rhetoric. Their most nonsensical threats—lacing the drinking water with LSD, and "turning on" the entire city; using Yippie girls to seduce conventioneers; the take-over of the entire city—were snapped up by at least some elements of the press. The *Tribune*-owned *American* went on an almost daily binge of eye-popping headlines and stories about the plans to disrupt the convention, taking every threat literally and seriously. Any pot-smoking adolescent with a mimeograph machine could count on a story. The *Tribune* itself sniffed around for the great Communist conspiracy it suspected of backing the pro-testers. It has one reporter who does nothing but ferret out supposed left-wing involvement in the membership of any organization the *Tribune* dislikes. The police Red Squad was snatching up every silly rumor as fact, passing it on to the *Tribune* papers, which printed them, and the city and rank-and-file policemen read them and became even more fearful. The other two papers, the *Daily News* and the *Sun-Times,* had reporters covering the New Left and dismissed most of the threats. By the beginning of con-vention week they had an accurate picture of how many demonstrators to expect, and were less inclined to get ex-cited.

Meanwhile, City Hall was playing its game of delay and stall on the requests for permits from the various groups that wanted to hold demonstrations and marches during convention week. As the convention drew near, there was no agreement. The city was firm in its denial of permits that would allow the marchers anywhere within miles of the convention Amphitheatre. It also refused to allow the protesters to sleep in the parks, although the 11 P.M. cur-few had been loosely enforced in the past. Boy Scouts had been given permission every year. People from the older neighborhoods slept in parks on hot nights. The pro-testers went to federal court in an effort to force the city to issue the various permits, but were turned down by Judge Lynch, Daley's hard-drinking old law partner, whom he had elevated to the federal bench.

In Washington, the Justice Department could see the threat of trouble building. Ramsey Clark, then attorney general, was convinced that Daley was overestimating the number of protesters coming to Chicago and their potential for mischief, and he was opposed to the massive show of force planned by Daley. But Daley was dealing directly with President Johnson, who shared his fears, and had been promised a sizable military force for the convention. Clark, however, sent two assistants to Chicago to try to shake Daley loose from his inflexible position: Wesley Pomeroy, who was in charge of coordinating federal and local law enforcement, and Roger Wilkins. Pomeroy said of the meeting:

"Our purpose each time was to persuade either Daley or his staff to begin negotiations with the leaders of the National Mobilization Committee to End the War in Viet Nam. Rennie Davis had communicated with Roger Wilkins that he was getting nowhere in trying to get permits and parade routes and he wanted some help so they could have some definite arrangements for a large number of people. They were talking about one hundred thousand people, but we didn't think that was likely. But Roger Wilkins had written a memo to Attorney General Clark saying that unless permits were granted and ground rules established, the likelihood of violence was extremely high. I wrote a memo endorsing what Roger had to say. It was my judgment that there needed to be negotiations. Experience has taught us in law enforcement that this is a reasonable way to plan for prevention of civil disorder.

"At our first meeting on July 25, we said we were offering all the assistance of the federal government to help him out. We were doing the same thing at the Republican Convention and we suggested it would be in the interest of Chicago to negotiate and work out ground rules.

"Daley said that the people in city government were already talking to the demonstrators and he said that if the Justice Department wanted to help, they should keep better track of the agitators and let him know when they were coming to Chicago so the police would be better prepared. He said that if there was any disorder here, he was sure it would be outside people causing it, not Chicagoans.

That was the substance of it. After we left, Roger asked me what I thought. I told him, 'You're better off if you both talk different languages; then you're sure you know you are not communicating.' There was simply no communication at that meeting.

"We reported to the attorney general and he was sorry we hadn't accomplished anything and agreed that it was absolutely essential that we do. The second time we met with Daley, I went with Warren Christopher, the deputy attorney general. Tom Foran, the U.S. attorney for northern Illinois, was with us, and the results were the same. Daley kept telling us that he'd take care of the dissenters. The only difference between the two meetings was that I had the feeling he disliked Roger Wilkins more than Warren Christopher."

Daley was not too worried about the antiwar groups. Their past exploits had shown them to be word warriors, and while their talk of open sexuality revolted him, he didn't fear them. His chief concern was the possibility of a black uprising. "You could see it all summer," said Ald. Leon Despres, an independent liberal. "He was running around the city constantly trying to give the impression of doing things for the black communities. He'd show up at dedications for the most minor of projects."

The police were applying pressure to black militants and to the ever-growing black youth gangs, making arrests whenever possible and harassing them on sight. By the time the convention began, many of the militants and gang leaders had left town, knowing that if anything happened, they'd be arrested immediately. The civil rights leaders cooled their followers. They wanted nothing to do with the war protest element, especially the Yippie types.

In Daley's zeal to keep the blacks quiet, even the name of the despised Dr. King was used for public relations benefits. On August 1, the City Council met to name a city street after him. They had chosen South Park Boulevard, which is almost entirely in the South Side black belt. Daley rejected suggestions that a city-length street be chosen, a street that would span both white and black neighborhoods, because he knew white residents would deface or remove the street signs. The meeting was remarkable, with one administration alderman after another eulogizing King as a great man, forgetting that they had assailed him when he was alive. Daley himself described his relationship with King as one of great friendship and mutual understanding, claiming that King had told him what a fine job he was doing for the city's blacks. The heights to which Daley and the aldermen rose in praising King moved one observer to write: "It was enough to bring tears to your eyes, if you happened to be a crocodile."

By the time the convention began, the most massive security arrangements in the history of American politics had been completed: Chicago's twelve thousand policemen had been put on twelve-hour shifts; five thousand Illinois national guardsmen had been mobilized and were standing by near the downtown area; six thousand specially trained army troops were flown in and were in combat readiness at the Glenview Naval Air Station, just north of the city; several hundred state and county lawmen were on call; and the largest number of secret service agents ever used at a political convention were in Chicago. Including the private security workers hired for the Amphitheatre, a defense force of at least twenty-five thousand was in Chicago. Daley had an army that was bigger than that commanded by George Washington. Never before had so many feared so much from so few.

At most, five thousand war protesters had come to Chicago. Daley's tough stance had terrified most of the hippies to the point where Chicago's long-hairs were warning their national brethren to stay away. Most of the straight protesters also decided to sit out Chicago. The message of the April 27 police assault on war protesters had sunk in. Of the five thousand, only a few hundred could have been labeled as revolutionaries, and most of these were known to investigators and their organizations thoroughly infiltrated. Anyone who even looked like a protest leader had a police tail. Some, such as Rennie Davis, were under such tight surveillance that they used their tails as drivers. The potential ineffectuality of this piddling gathering was heightened by their divergent politics, their inclination not to follow leaders, and the lack of leadership. As a disruptive force, their only weapons were words and the stunts devised for the TV camera. During the week before the convention, some staged a bumbling karate training class in Lincoln Park and practiced a laughable "snake dance," a defensive tactic used by Japanese students to break away from police attacks.

Delegates, almost forgotten as participants in the convention because of the mounting hysteria over the protesters, were arriving, many of them angered by the security arrangements. They were also amused by Daley's "redwood forest"—wooden fences he had erected along the route from the Loop to the Amphitheatre to conceal unsightly buildings and the rubble of empty lots.

There could be no mistake about whose city they were in. From the airport to their hotels, the name was everywhere: "Mayor Daley Welcomes You to Chicago . . . You Have Arrived in Daley Country . . ." When they picked up the phone next to their beds, his face, on a card pasted to the phone's cradle, smiled up at them. "Welcome," it said, "Richard J. Daley, Mayor." Theater marquees, store windows were all plastered with his name. And everywhere were policemen in blue-helmeted riot gear.

The city a secure armed camp, Daley was enjoying himself and the glow of the limelight. On Sunday he brought the Illinois delegation into caucus and for two hours they made speeches in praise of him, finally electing him their chairman. Then they heard from the candidates: Vice-President Humphrey, Senators Eugene McCarthy and George McGovern, and finally Gov. Lester Maddox, of Georgia. Maddox was in the middle of a long, rambling speech about the paving of roads when Daley leaned over, tugged his coat, and said, "Say, Gov, can you wind it up? The wives are waiting and we have a party scheduled." Then Daley surprised everyone by postponing the Illinois delegation's vote until Wednesday instead of polling them in the beginning and coming out for Humphrey, as he had been expected to do.

With Johnson's decision not to seek renomination, and with the assassination of Sen. Robert Kennedy, it had been assumed that Daley was prepared to support Vice-President Humphrey. McCarthy, with his unpredictability, and the relatively unknown McGovern were not his kind of candidate. However, Daley, as he later admitted, wasn't enthusiastic about Humphrey. He looked like a loser, at least in Illinois, and Daley was concerned about getting a candidate who would, above all, help his state and county ticket. To Daley, that candidate was the sole surviving Kennedy brother. He delayed the Illinois caucus in hopes that Sen. Edward Kennedy would either be persuaded to declare himself a candidate or that a draft could be generated. Daley, however, did not want to lead the draft, and Kennedy could not be persuaded to take the first step by announcing his availability. "Daley wanted him, sure," said Alderman Keane. "I was there when the mayor talked to him on the phone. I don't know if Kennedy would have won, but it would have kept him out of trouble."

The postponement of his choice heightened interest in his role as "king maker." When he didn't make his move on Sunday, backers of the candidates began courting him more intensely. But even the Illinois delegation was kept in the dark as to Daley's planning. Except for his small circle of intimates among the delegates, the others weren't sure where he, and therefore they, stood. If the convention had been run normally, Daley could have played his party-leader role to the brim of his ego. But the action developing on the streets was making him more memorable as a head breaker than as a king maker.

On Sunday, about four thousand people, at most, gathered in Lincoln Park, which is on the lake front about two miles north of the Loop and eight miles north of the Amphitheatre. They were a mixed group, predominantly young, but with a sizable number of older people from the nearby Old Town area. Old Town, one of the city's more colorful areas, is made up of excellently renovated old homes and small apartment buildings with a large population of business, professional, and artistic people. Wells Street, the original home of Chicago hippies and later a tourist attraction, with its restaurants, bars, and boutiques, ends at Lincoln Park. On an ordinary summer weekend, crowded Lincoln Park doesn't look much different than it did when the convention was beginning. The big difference was the large number of helmeted policemen.

During the afternoon, several hundred protesters had marched downtown to take part in a peaceful rally. The handful of tough radical agitators were taunting the police in the park and trying to generate excitement, but most of the crowd was decidedly nonviolent. A few minor skirmishes had broken out between police and radicals, but most of the people had spent the day listening to rock music, orators, and in conversation.

That Sunday night, the convention, so far as most of the world would be concerned, began. The issue was as simple as a child's game of king-of-the-hill. The protesters were in the park. The city ordinance required that the park had to be vacated by eleven o'clock. This is what may have determined the election and altered the course of world history—the decision of the city that nobody would be in Lincoln Park after eleven o'clock.

The police, and the city's lawyers who directed them, had the law on their side. But, as a practical matter, the decision to clear the park at night was bereft of logic. From the city's point of view, the protesters could not have picked a better place to camp than in Lincoln Park.

To the north was more park and the Lincoln Park Zoo. To the east was Lake Shore Drive and the beaches. To the south was park and a huge high-rise development. And from Stockton Drive, the other border, the protesters were not even visible in the darkness. If the city had been able to choose a place to put the protesters to isolate them from the rest of the city and the convention, to watch them, they couldn't have picked a better site than that chosen by the protesters themselves.

Only one thousand or so people remained in the darkness of Lincoln Park by midnight Sunday. Others had gone on a noisy but nondisruptive march up Michigan Avenue. Some had left the park in small, chanting groups and were quickly scattered by the police. But most of the earlier crowd of four thousand had left to get some sleep. At this point the police had the tactical and psychological advantage. Those who remained were chilly, nervous, and unsure of what the police would do. If the police had waited and done nothing, the militants would have had to force the confrontation on them—and it is unlikely they could have dragged the middle-road majority with them. And if they didn't leave the park to seek a police confrontation, they would have sat through the chilly, damp night, in which case most of them would have probably left before dawn.

Instead, the city forced the confrontation and the police became the aggressors, striking out at militant and middle-roaders alike, involving thousands of people in the violence, and making the dominant event of the convention a battle over a few acres of grassland.

The police made their first sweep through the park, moving from the east toward the streets, shedding whatever discipline they had shown earlier in the day. They beat people beyond the point of subduing them. They chased them down and left them bleeding.

The first chilling scene of a reporter being forced to surrender his notebook, a photographer his film, unfolded. A *Newsweek* reporter, press credentials pinned to his coat and not interfering with police, was coolly and systematically beaten. A Philadelphia newsman was told, "Hey, you dirty bastard, give me that goddamn notebook," by a policeman who had been jabbing a girl with his nightstick. As he surrendered his notebook, the policeman clubbed him and left him bloody.

Seven newsmen were attacked by police that night. In only one case could there have been any mistake made about the person's identity. It was clear the police were looking for reporters, that they were prime targets.

One reason for mistreating reporters was the police's desire to have their overall brutality go unrecorded. But beyond that, the press was part of the enemy. Since 1960, when they had been humiliated by the Summerdale police scandal, Chicago police had nursed a grudge. It was the press that later seemed to always side with the blacks, informing on police who committed excesses. Add to that the fact that many of the reporters covering the street action were young, some modishly dressed and with long hair, some black, and the police attacks were explainable. After Sunday night, some policemen warned their friends among Chicago reporters to be careful, that the word was out to get the press.

Daley, who shared the police's distrust of reporters, supported the attacks by claiming that they were not serious and no fault of the police. This was his way of getting the message across. He said, "They think because they're working for a newspaper that they can do anything, they can violate any law, they can take any action because they are newsmen. This shouldn't be. This isn't any prerogative of newsmen, television or radio or anyone else."

On Monday the police violence increased. Fighting broke out at a rally in Grant Park, along Michigan Avenue, near the hotels where most of the delegates were staying. And that night the police again chose to clear Lincoln Park, waiting until after midnight to do so, rejecting the tactical options as they had done on Sunday night, and loping through the park with chants of "kill, kill, kill." By Monday night it was irrelevant to the police whether the person they clubbed was young or old, male or female, a protester or a hapless neighborhood resident who happened to be on his way home from work.

Clergymen trying to calm the situation were beaten. Some people were tossed into the park's lagoon, including a man who was going home on a bike. Police beat people many blocks from the park, invaded a couple of homes, sprayed Mace into the shocked faces of residents who leaned out of their windows to look, and proved with their cries of "kill the motherfuckers" that the Yippies had no copyright on gutter language.

That night, scores of people were beaten badly enough to require hospital treatment, including twenty newsmen. After Sunday's jolting experience, reporters had mistakenly taken to wearing even bigger press credentials, which only served to attract the police like hungry sharks. The confiscation of film increased, and several cameras were damaged.

Angered, finally, the editors of papers and magazines flooded Daley with written protests. But he jutted out his chin and refused even to acknowledge the reality of the Lincoln Park beatings. "How can policemen tell the difference between a demonstrator and a newsman?" he demanded.

The tempers at the Amphitheatre were as short, if not as violent, as those in the streets. The security agents hounded delegates and newsmen, and one TV interviewer was punched in the stomach on the convention floor. Yet Daley remained outwardly serene, sometimes buoyant, while all around him the tension was building. In the parks his policemen were undergoing what, most charitably, could be called temporary insanity. To a nation and a world, his Chicago was beginning to look like a madhouse, and the famous TV commentators were being blunt about it. By Wednesday, there was more interest in Daley and his policemen than in the expected nomination of Humphrey.

The famous battle of Michigan Avenue was fought in front of the Hilton on Wednesday night, with mass clubbings, people shoved through broken restaurant windows, chased into the lobby of the hotel, and all of it captured on television in one of the most dramatic moments in the history of the medium.

While it was happening, Daley sat in his delegate's chair, with son Richard to his left and Tom Keane behind him, trying to participate in a convention as if nothing happening on the street was in any way connected with it. That was the way he wanted everybody to look at it: let my police take care of the business in the street. We are here to take care of party matters, to choose a candidate for president. But word of the bloodbath had reached the convention hall, and, after three days of frustration, the anger of many delegates boiled over. The chairman of the Colorado delegation interrupted the proceedings to say: "Is there any rule under which Mayor Daley can be compelled to suspend the police state terror being perpetrated at this minute on kids in front of the Conrad Hilton?" Son Richard and other Illinois delegates turned and bellowed insults at him.

Then came one of the most raucous exchanges of the convention. Sen. Abraham Ribicoff stepped to the rostrum to nominate Senator McGovern for president, and he said, "If we had McGovern, we wouldn't have the Gestapo in the streets of Chicago." Members of the Illinois delegation jumped up and began gesturing for McGovern to get off the platform, making thumbs-down motions. Ribicoff went on, saying, "How hard it is to accept the truth, how hard it is."

"The thing that got Daley mad," one of the delegates said later, "was that Ribicoff had been ass-kissing him just a day or two before. He came over and pushed for

McGovern to our delegation and made a big speech about what a great guy Daley was. Then he got up there and played the hero for the TV cameras."

Daley was on his feet, his arms waving, his mouth working. The words were lost in the uproar, but it was later asserted by *Mayday,* an almost-underground Washington paper, that a lip-reader had determined that he said: "Fuck you, you Jew son of a bitch, you lousy motherfucker, go home."

"Absolutely not," said Alderman Keane, who claimed to have heard everything Daley said. "He just said go home."

Patricia Moore, the society editor of the *Chicago Daily News,* was in the press section and said she had a clear view of Daley's face. "I was watching him closely," Miss Moore said, "and his lips definitely formed the word 'fuck.' "

George Dunne, the soft-spoken president of the Cook County Board, said firmly that no obscenities had been shouted, but he offered an explanation for why people thought they had been. "Daley and a lot of us were shouting 'faker, faker.' That's because of his presentation to our delegation and because we thought he was just making a show for his home state. If you move your lips to form 'faker,' it looks just like you're saying that other thing."

"I didn't hear what Daley said," said Ald. Seymour Simon, a member of the Illinois delegation and a Jew, "but others were yelling things like 'go home you dirty kike, you dirty agitator, Communist.' "

Daley later contributed to the debate over what he called Ribicoff, although he wouldn't clear up the mystery. A reporter at a press conference quoted the *Mayday* report, and Daley screamed, "You're a liar. Don't say that. I never used that language in my life, and you say that or anything else and you lie, you're a liar."

At the moment he shouted whatever it was that he shouted, the exact words didn't matter. But the tone, the quality, of the convention did, and it had settled to the level of Daley politics, Bridgeport politics, and Chicago politics. He was on his feet telling them off, letting them know that they couldn't push him around, giving it back blow for blow, insult for insult. The press had tried it

and now they were getting theirs. The outside trouble-
makers came looking for trouble, and he gave it to them.
Now Ribicoff and the others were giving him lip, and he
was telling them where they could go.

But for once, it was he who was shouted down. After
Ribicoff came Frank Mankiewicz, a former Kennedy aide,
to second McGovern and assail the "mindless brutality
on Chicago streets and on this convention floor."

The feelings in the hall were so intense that a wall of
security men had moved around the Illinois delegation. A
Michigan delegate got through and tried to reason with
Daley about the police conduct. Daley brushed him off.
An Illinois Democrat did the same. Daley listened, said
"thank you," and turned away. A Wisconsin delegate
offered a motion to adjourn the convention and move it
to another city. The contempt for Daley was pouring down
from all directions. He tried to maintain an outward indifference by chatting casually with members of his group.
But inwardly he was shaken, and it showed when Illinois'
turn came to place candidates in nomination. Daley was
so rattled that he got up and, instead of making a nomination, he announced Illinois' delegate vote for Humphrey.
Then, behind a phalanx of guards, he left the floor and
the building for the night. When the convention finally
selected Humphrey to be its candidate, Daley, the host,
the man who brought the convention to his city, the "king
maker," wasn't in the convention hall.

He went to a nearby hotel suite and sat in front of the
television set watching the replay of the Michigan Avenue
club swinging, seeing for himself, finally, that which he
had denied was happening. The "battle of Balbo" was no
more vicious than the police attacks in Lincoln Park and
on the streets of Old Town, but it was the only one
captured fully by television. Now much of the world had
seen it, so he could no longer deny that it was happening,
or claim that the reports were being exaggerated. Now he
had to somehow justify it.

The next day, he had his new strategy. He surprised
CBS by telling them that he was available to be interviewed by Walter Cronkite. Cronkite was unprepared for
the stunning disclosures made by Daley in justifying the
massive show of police force.

"Let me say something I never said to anyone. It's unfortunate . . . but the television industry didn't have the information I had. There were reports and intelligence on my desk that certain people planned to assassinate the three contenders for the presidency; that certain people planned to assassinate many of the leaders, including myself. So I took the necessary precautions."

There was his answer, his justification, his way out for the moment. Now it could be told. Those supposedly innocent people out there getting clubbed—among them was a cold-eyed assassin, maybe a ring of cold-eyed assassins. Shades of JFK, RFK, and Dr. King. No wonder the police were fighting so mightily: the leadership of the nation was in the crosshairs. And there sat this man from Bridgeport, this family man, this hard-working, misunderstood man, finally unburdening himself of that which he had stoically endured in silence: somebody out there planned to kill him and just about everybody else of importance at the convention. And the news media, in its ignorance of the truth, and the facts, had been blaming him, when all along they should have been pinning medals on him. Now, who could blame a man for taking strong, decisive measures in the face of deadly threats? Who could fault him for doing what had to be done to protect the lives of potential presidents? Did Walter Cronkite have any "reports and intelligence" on his desk? Or Huntley or Brinkley, or anybody else? You bet they didn't. But he did. And who would dispute "reports and intelligence"? Millions of people in the TV audience wouldn't.

It was an effective ploy because nobody could dispute it, at least immediately, and Daley knew that the impressions made during the convention were those that would harden and endure. His story might be poked full of holes in the future, but that didn't matter.

Daley, as it turned out, seemed to be the only person who knew about an assassination plot. Later, the head of the Chicago FBI office said he didn't remember any plot against Daley. Earl Bush, the mayor's trusted press aide, said the first he knew about it was when Daley blurted it out on Cronkite's show. U.S. Attorney Foran said there had been rumors, started by some prisoners who were locked up in the Cook County jail, but nothing that was substantiated. Another high-ranking federal official said flatly, "There was nothing to it. The whole thing was as whispy as a dream."

Further proof of the absence of an assassination plot came when a federal grand jury indicted the main figures in the so-called Conspiracy Eight trial. Presumably, the grand jury would have been as interested in a conspiracy to assassinate prominent officials as they were in the alleged conspiracy to cross state lines to incite riot. But a death-conspiracy wasn't even included in the list of possible offenses the grand jury was asked to investigate.

As to the "reports and intelligence" that were on Daley's desk, he never said what they contained, where they came from, or what happened to them. They were never mentioned again. But on Thursday of convention week, they made a good story and helped him launch a counteroffensive. He had been humiliated Wednesday night and that could not go unanswered. On Thursday the word went out to precinct captains in Bridgeport and several other South Side wards that each of them should bring ten people to ward headquarters. They were loaded on buses, given "Daley" signs, noisemakers, and special oversized passes to the gallery. Daley was going to pull the oldest convention stunt of them all—packing the gallery. It was a strange time to do it, since the choice of a candidate for President had already been made, but he was packing the gallery for himself. Now, if there was anybody shouted down, his people would do the shouting.

That night, when he entered the hall, the chant "We love Daley, we love Daley," rolled down from the gallery, most of it filled with his patronage workers. Throughout the evening, he turned them on and off like an orchestra conductor. After seeing a film about Sen. Robert Kennedy, delegates emotionally sang the "Battle Hymn of the Republic," until Daley thought it was time to stop and he used his gallery to drown out the singing. The New Hampshire delegation tried to make speeches about the arrest of their chairman, who had been collared and taken to Daley's neighborhood police station when he tried to show that the hall's ID checkers were rigged, but their words were lost in the chants of Daley's gallery. Wisconsin nominated Julian Bond for vice-president and Daley, to cut off the speeches, gleefully led the gallery in singing "God Bless America." This was his night, and throughout, his eyes gleamed and he laughed joyously at the discomfiture of his enemies.

He stopped laughing, though, when Bull Connor, the former Birmingham police chief, cast his vote for vice-president for Daley. Nothing his liberal critics said could have put the situation more clearly than did Connor's one vote. The man who had risen from political mediocrity by identifying with Adlai Stevenson, Sen. Paul Douglas, and other progressive elements of the party, the man who had been hailed as a new kind of mayor, had become the new symbol of repression. Connor, an old symbol, had passed him the torch.

Then it was over. On Friday the Democratic party limped out of Chicago. Humphrey and Senator Muskie were the ticket, but all that anybody remembered was Daley and his city. He had wanted to be the center of attention, and he was. One of the New England delegations sent him a telegram from New York and said they were glad to be out of Chicago and back in the free world. Editorials from all over the country and much of Europe were pointing at him as being a neofascist. Even one of his lieutenants, U.S. Rep. Roman Pucinski, a backlash representative from the white Northwest Side, unwittingly summed up Daley's impact on the party when he tried to praise him by saying, "We survived the Chicago fire; we will survive this."

With Daley, it was more than a matter of survival. He wanted vindication. He wanted history to show that he had been right, and his critics and opponents had been wrong, so he set out to write a history that way.

In only a week, his staff produced the city's "official" report on the convention, titled "Strategy on Confrontation." Through omissions, half-truths and outright lies, the rambling report placed the entire blame on the peace protesters and the news media. The newspapers printed most or all of the report, without simultaneous rebuttal, despite bitter protests by the reporters who had covered the events and were eager to poke holes into Daley's version. One newspaper executive later explained that his paper did not challenge the report and even printed it as a special supplement that could be used as a mail-out to out-of-town friends, because: "Chicago was under attack all over the world and we felt it had to be defended."

Daley also hired a television producer to create a TV special of the city's version. But even in that blatant attempt to place all the blame on "outsiders" and exonerate the police, the hired producers were unable to include in the special any of the alleged attacks on police that supposedly provoked them to violence. The producer had access to police department films which, presumably, would have included such attacks if they had occurred.

The propaganda served only to solidify opinion, not to change minds. Surveys taken immediately after the convention established that most people polled thought Daley and his police had been correct. Daley said his mail supported his approach. In attacking the young, the liberal, and the black, Daley was in the mainstream of America's mass prejudices. The Democratic party may have suffered by his actions, but Daley came out of the convention even more popular than before because "bust their heads" was the mood of the land and Daley had swung the biggest club. The conservative Timothy Sheehan, Cook County Republican chairman and Daley's opponent for mayor in 1959, said, "I used to be able to get a rise out of any downstate or suburban audience by mentioning 'Boss Daley' or 'Dictator Dick' and his one-man rule. That always worked them up. But after 1968, that didn't work out there anymore. They like Daley in the most conservative areas, and they should. Nobody did the job he did. He didn't let the minority groups have whatever they wanted. He took a stand."

As the election approached, it was every man for himself. After the chaos of Daley's convention, it took Humphrey weeks to get his campaign effectively underway and to begin moving up in the preelection polls. But by then, convinced that Humphrey was a loser, Daley's Machine concentrated on the local ticket, especially the office of state's attorney. Precinct captains in the backlash neighborhoods explained to voters how they could split their ticket and vote for Wallace while also voting for the Machine's local candidates. The precinct captains weren't chanting it the way the protesters did on Michigan

Avenue, but the movement to "Dump the Hump" was just as real. Humphrey made a last-ditch swing through Illinois and into Chicago for a parade and a rally, but the usually efficient Machine did a sloppy job in providing a turnout.

Nixon took Illinois, and Republican Richard Ogilvie, once again running against a surprisingly weak candidate chosen by Daley, was elected governor. The Republicans also won the state office of attorney general. Daley's great kingdom had shrunk overnight to the borders of Cook County, and he no longer had a friend in the White House.

Nixon's victory was not a landslide. In fact, it appeared that if Humphrey had not been dismissed by the Machine as being hopeless and an effort had been made, he might have taken Illinois. In Cook County, Edward Hanrahan, Daley's candidate for state's attorney, ran two hundred thousand votes ahead of Humphrey, which was the state-wide margin by which Nixon won.

One of the keys to the Republican victory was the black vote. In a quiet way, many black voters rebelled against Daley's man-handling of them by sitting out the election. They voted Democratic, but in fewer numbers than in past general elections. A dozen black wards that had produced 312,000 votes in 1960, and 341,000 in 1964, turned out only 243,000 votes in 1968. The drop in the black vote was estimated to be more than one hundred thousand.

One high-ranking Machine leader placed the blame for the 1968 losses on Daley. "The stuff about the invincibility of the Daley Machine is just so much bullshit. What's so invincible when you lose offices like governor and you don't have a senator, and you lose county offices? The only thing invincible about the Machine is that it gets him elected. We lost in '68 because we didn't get the black vote. In the white backlash wards, they turned out ninety-two percent of the registered voters, but only seventy-two percent of the black vote came out. If we had the black vote the way we should have, we would have won it all."

Daley blamed Humphrey for his defeat in Illinois. After the election, Humphrey made remarks to the effect that the convention debacle had damaged his chances, and Daley angrily responded. "I thought we had a stronger candidate [in Edward Kennedy]. We should have had a stronger candidate. [Humphrey] was defeated because he didn't visit downstate. He was asked to come in repeatedly, but all he did was spend thirty minutes in Rockford and a half hour in Chicago."

Daley also found surprising new scapegoats for the convention disorders—Humphrey and the Johnson administration. "It wasn't the people of Chicago who brought those people (the protesters) here. It was the candidacy of Humphrey and the policies of the administration on Vietnam. We had nothing to do with that." Daley conveniently forgot that he had been one of the loudest and most consistent supporters of the Johnson Vietnam policies.

His Police Department's Intelligence Division had constantly harassed peace groups, going so far as to burglarize their offices and rifle files. Whether it was mere party loyalty or his personal belief, Daley's repeated statements in support of the Vietnam involvement had branded him as a hawk.

His hawkishness had been an unlikely role, since neither Daley nor the rest of his family had shown any taste for the realities of war. He was thirty-nine when World War II broke out, and while other men his age or older volunteered, he did not.

At the time when his hawkish views were most pronounced, none of Daley's four draft-age, able-bodied, athletic, and healthy sons served on active military duty. All had avoided Vietnam through the socially acceptable evasion of the draft—joining a reserve unit. One of them, in fact, was accepted by a local reserve unit when there was a waiting list of several thousand applicants, although he had not been on the waiting list.

The Daley tradition of noninvolvement in the actual shooting made even more ironic his remarks to a Chicago-area promilitary group honoring General Westmoreland not long after the convention. Daley said:

"We're honored, our city is honored, to have such a fine and outstanding example of the military of our fine country. We're proud of them and everyone should be proud of them and those who are not proud of them should get out of the country if they don't like it."

Or join a reserve unit, he might have added.

As the debate raged on for months after the election, the strain of the turbulent year began to show on Daley. He looked haggard and could no longer go through a full day of work without showing fatigue. At times his head would nod sleepily at formal dinners, and he lost the thread of conversations. One night an old friend was leaving the Tavern Club, a quiet private dining club in a high-rise on Michigan Avenue, when he noticed Daley and his wife sitting alone at a table in a corner.

"I stopped to say hello, and I couldn't believe the shape he was in. His eyes were glassy and he seemed barely able to keep them open. We talked for a couple of minutes, but I couldn't understand what he was saying, that's how slurred his speech was. I thought that he was drunk, but then I realized it was exhaustion. He seemed to be out on his feet. I'm sure that the shape he was in, all it would take is one or two drinks to put him away."

Some of his intimates were seriously concerned with his health. A case of what began as simple flu kept him home for ten days, the longest absence due to illness in his career as mayor. Dr. Eric Oldberg, president of the Board of Health, said of the flu bout: "He was teetering on the brink of something serious. He was very weak. His weight was up. His EKG [electrocardiogram] was not good. He was in very bad shape."

But the Daley stamina and physical toughness that helped both his parents live to old age brought him back, as belligerent and unyielding as ever. The President's Commission on Violence had studied the Chicago convention, and the result was the scathing Walker Report, prepared by Daniel Walker, a top-drawer business executive with full Establishment credentials, and his staff of some thirty-five investigators. It was a thorough study of the events leading to the convention and the violence of the week, and it found that much of the violence was the result of "police riot." Adlai Stevenson III, emerging as the temporary standard-bearer for the outraged liberal wing of the party, and probably the one man, thanks to his famous name, who could seriously challenge the Machine for office in a primary election, lashed at Daley as a "feudal boss." Daley conceded nothing.

"I say again, and I am proud of it, there was no one killed in Chicago and no one shot in Chicago. . . . The American public was defrauded by television coverage of the convention . . . stations set up what happened at Michigan and Balboa and everybody knows it . . . we didn't create the turbulence. Everybody knows television forced it. There wasn't a fair presentation of the news. I had nothing to do with setting up the convention or with running the Police Department . . . Daley gave no orders to the Police Department. I defy anyone to show that I did. No one runs the Police Department but Superintendent Conlisk . . ."

Regardless of what the Walker Report, the liberals, the critics of his methods might say, Daley knew what most people were saying: he was right. The political winds were blowing from the right, and he was as much a part of it as Wallace, Agnew, or Strom Thurmond. He didn't have to apologize for anything he had done, and it was almost a year later that he said, in a speech to a conservative group that cheered him wildly:

"Someone asked me a few days ago, would you do over what you did in August? And in the true tradition of the Gaelic spirit of the Daleys, I said: 'You're damn right I'd do the same thing, only with greater effort.'"

Chapter X

KUNSTLER: Who is David Stahl? Do you know
   him?

WITNESS: He is a very fine young man, the
   deputy mayor. . . . He was a former vice-
   president of one of the outstanding corpora-
   tions in Chicago and he is doing an outstanding job for the people of our city.

KUNSTLER: I will assume with all of the people
   I ask about that they are very fine young
   men and so on. It will save time.

WITNESS: I would say that anyone that serves
   in government today is a fine young man
   because of what we are trying to do.

The black limousine pulls in front of the house and waits
for him. It is another workday for most of the city, but
down at City Hall, it will be something special. The
moment he strides in from Washington Boulevard, the
cry of "Happy birthday, Mr. Mayor" will ring out, to be
repeated hundreds of times throughout the day.

   The arrangements are always the same. At about ten
o'clock, a baker will wheel a giant cake into the fifth-
floor conference room, the TV crews will set up their
equipment, the whiz kids from his staff will file in, followed

by the big men in the Machine and the lesser known old-
timers from around the building who go way back with
him. When everyone has arrived, the bodyguards will
scan the gathering for unfamiliar faces.

Given the all clear, he will enter, shaking hands, accepting the congratulations for another year of life, another year of success, another year of power. After slicing
the cake for the cameramen, he will step to the microphones for his usual birthday observations. They are always the same because his values do not change. He
speaks of his good fortune in having God-fearing, honest,
hard-working parents, his fine neighborhood and loyal
friends, his devoted family. Then he talks of the accomplishments of his administration, the works of his political
party, and finally of his goals for the city.

These being the essential ingredients of his life and
career, his sixty-eighth birthday, on May 15, 1970, should
have been most enjoyable. In many ways it should have
been the most satisfying celebration of his years in public
office. It should have been a good ride downtown, through
his city.

He had those things that would be important to any
man at sixty-eight, regardless of whether he was a mayor
or a miner. His health was good, his hand steady. With
his help, his sons were marching in his footsteps toward
their own careers in law and politics. His daughters had
married and brought him grandchildren. Many of his old
friends were gone, but others survived, men with whom he
could look back to the times when they were humble
unknowns.

Beyond that, there was his career, which meant the city
and the Machine. They still belonged to him. At sixty-
eight, an age when other men were cashing pension
checks, he was still running things, and it was no longer
a matter of distant goals, of proving himself, of finding
his place in history: he had shaped the city and Machine
to his liking. If it ended right there, he could say he had
done all of the big things. Now it was simply a matter of
doing more of them. Despite the angry bleatings from the
nation's liberals, who had actually demanded and expected
that he be destroyed, dethroned, punished by the Chicago
voters, he was still there. They didn't know him and they

didn't know Chicago. He had put everything and everyone in their proper places.

His Machine, threatened after the convention by a revolt of liberals, independents, and blacks, had been tightened and was again running smoothly. He had disabled them with one smooth gesture.

Their plan had been to run independent slates against his men in the 1970 county and state primaries, and even against him in the 1971 election for mayor. Their leader, or so they had hoped, was to be Aldai Stevenson III, the state treasurer and the only person who had the name and vote power to lead an anti-Machine movement. Stevenson sounded, at times, as if he were considering the role. After the Democratic Convention, he had lashed at Daley for exercising "feudal" political leadership. And without committing himself, he listened to the dissidents.

But when the unbeatable Sen. Everett M. Dirksen died in late 1969, Daley offered Stevenson the chance to run against Dirksen's nondescript replacement, and Stevenson hastily accepted the Machine's support, and offered its candidates his loyalty. As one of his liberal supporters wryly put it: "True, Adlai said Daley was a feudal boss, but he didn't say he was a bad feudal boss." By slating Stevenson, whom he personally disliked, Daley couldn't lose. If Stevenson was elected, he'd be off to Washington and out of Daley's hair. If he lost, he'd be a young has-been. And without Stevenson's name as their banner, the rebellious factions remained splintered and interesting only to themselves.

While using Stevenson to retrieve liberal support for the party, Daley managed the almost miraculous feat of simultaneously finding a new law-and-order symbol to beat off the threat of rising Republican strength in the 1970 fall elections. And his new symbol sprang from the best of all sources—an old Machine family.

Richard Elrod, at thirty-six, had been just one of the many trusted, second-generation political creatures who were elbowing their way through the pack to the secondary political offices and jobs. His father, Artie, had been the last of the white committeemen of the legendary Twenty-fourth Ward organization, succeeding Jacob

Arvey. The elder Elrod was a classic ward boss, with a
background in tavern-keeping, gambling, bail bonding,
real estate, insurance, and a circle of friends that included
some of the better-known West Side gangsters. When he
died wealthy, he was one of the more important members
of the Cook County Board of Commissioners.

His son, Richard, was a model of Machine upward
mobility. After Northwestern University Law School, he
was given a job in the city's legal department and later
elected to the state legislature from an upper middle class
white district on the far North Side. As a city lawyer, he
became Daley's man at the scene of the demonstrations
and riots, advising police and gathering material for prosecution. And in 1969 the Weatherman faction of the
SDS made Elrod one of the city's greatest heroes by staging their "Days of Rage" that included a window-breaking
spree in the Loop in which Elrod was seriously injured,
suffering paralysis from the neck down. The police
promptly disclosed that one of the Weahterman members
had slugged Elrod with a lead pipe. For weeks, the papers
carried almost daily reports on his medical progress, disc
jockeys eulogized him and berated anyone to the political
left of Daley, and Elrod became a symbol of all that was
brave and good in Chicago life.

He was still in his hospital bed when Daley visited him
and asked him to run for sheriff. Elrod could campaign
in a wheel chair, and maybe by election he would be
walking. The Republicans had already slated a well-
qualified former FBI agent as their candidate for sheriff,
and under normal circumstances he would have beaten
Elrod. Under normal circumstances, in fact, Daley would
not have slated Elrod for sheriff. Although the Elrod
family had left the old West Side, they still had roots
there, including the ownership of slum-style properties.
There had even been a nasty court fight with the black
committeeman who succeeded Arthur Elrod over exclusive
rights to peddle insurance, a political booty, in the ward.

These weren't the most desirable credentials for a
sheriff candidate, but to stand a chance the Republican
ex-FBI man would have had to be shot by the Mafia or
stabbed by Abbie Hoffman. Later, factual accounts of
Elrod's injury came out at the trial of the accused attacker.

There had been no lead pipe. In fact, Elrod injured himself while throwing a wild flying tackle at the Weatherman, an exercise that wasn't part of his job. But by that time, the facts surrounding his injuries and his Machine background meant little to the voters. He was a law-and-order hero, and Daley had him on the ticket. Congressman Roman Pucinski summed it up at a Democratic rally, after Elrod walked slowly and stiffly across the stage: "It is a masterstroke." And it was. With Stevenson leading the way, the Machine swept all Cook County and state offices. The Democrats even took control of the Illinois Senate for the first time in 37 years. It was one of Daley's greatest victories.

The political dissenters weren't the only ones who had threatened Daley, only to be slapped down and brought into line. There was the case of the city's medical establishment and his friend, old "Doc" O'Connell.

Back in 1962, Dr. Morgan O'Connell had retired to Florida after a career in obstetrics that was distinguished only by his having brought the entire Daley brood into the world. During a vacation in Florida, the Daleys visited O'Connell and found him restless and unhappy in retirement, so Daley brought him back to Chicago and appointed him assistant city health commissioner. This brought protests from the socially prominent president of the city's Board of Health, Dr. Eric Oldberg, who had been trying to make the best of a public health agency that was a political dumping ground for overage, undertalented, and sometimes hard-drinking doctors. O'Connell, he pointed out, had no experience or degree in public health, both of which were required by law and good sense. But Daley soothingly assured him that his old friend O'Connell wouldn't be in the job for long, and need not be given any important responsibilities. "I just want to make the old man happy," Daley said. "He means a lot to my family."

Six years later the health commissioner quit during a minor scandal in the department, and Daley elevated O'Connell to the job of "acting commissioner." "Having the title will mean a lot to the old man," Daley told the amazed Oldberg. "I won't keep him there long," he added, promising to quickly find a qualified, experienced man.

At the time he bestowed the second ego-building honor on his wife's doctor, the city's TB rate was twice the national average; the city's infant mortality rate was climbing while the national rate was dropping, and in the black slum areas, the infant death rate was higher than in all but two nations in the developed world. Yet, Daley was capable of putting an unqualified man in charge.

It wasn't a surprise, public health not being something that can be seen from the airport buses, or photographed by a national magazine, or viewed as part of the skyline or the lake front image. The people who needed the public health facilities weren't the kind who were aware that they were being shortchanged. So under O'Connell, the already scarce neighborhood public health clinics were roach infested, filthy, understaffed. Puerto Rican children were arriving in Chicago without being met by an effective diphtheria program, an oversight that very nearly created an epidemic. Alcoholics needed political pull to get into the city's drunk treatment clinics. But Mrs. Daley's favorite doctor had a big title.

O'Connell seemed unaware that the health problems existed. When a severe flu epidemic hit and the city was caught short of serum, O'Connell simply announced that there was no flu epidemic: all those people were dying of old age, infancy, or pneumonia, he said, but not flu. When the pollution level soared for several days beyond the federally-designated danger level, prompting many doctors to send respiratory cases out of town, O'Connell said, "I don't believe there is that much. . . . Anyone who might experience problems is probably older." And when asked why he didn't try to ease the problem of malnutrition in the ghetto by taking advantage of a federal free food program for children and pregnant women, he said, "As I go around the city, I don't see any hungry people."

After a year, the city's medical leaders had had enough. A delegation from several hospitals and medical schools went to Daley's office and, after itemizing O'Connell's failings, demanded that he be replaced. For their efforts, they received a lesson in what the Machine was all about. Daley listened, then erupted in one of his purple-faced rages, ranting for a full fifteen minutes. "You say you represent the people," he shouted. "Well, where are they? Where are the mothers, where are the Negroes, where are the labor leaders?" He sent them away without even a hint of a promise that he would make a change. But he wasn't done with them. Furious, he taught them that nobody was telling him who he should hire and fire.

City inspectors moved in on some of the hospitals that had been represented at the meeting. One of the hospitals, an outstanding institution, had to put in a new hundred-thousand-dollar stairwell. Another was warned by O'Connell that he might close it down because it didn't have enough nurses. The warning came at a time when few hospitals could hire enough nurses to meet the city's prescribed nurse-patient ratio. Under this kind of pressure, the medical men backed off and kept quiet.

And Daley triumphantly removed the "acting" from O'Connell's title. His wife's old doctor finally had full honors, and also qualified for a sizable city pension. He would have remained on the job as long as Daley was mayor, too, if he hadn't made a blunder that even his old friend couldn't tolerate. O'Connell made the mistake of botching his budget-making procedures, bypassing the health board while sending his budget straight to City Hall. For this, but not his medical shortcomings, he was ordered to retire by Daley, always the meticulous bookkeeper.

He had slapped down the educational reformers, too, when they made the same mistake as the medical people: trying to tell him how to run things. That was why he had his own, obedient board running the school system, helping maintain its reputation as being among the very worst in the nation. Schools in the black areas could not have been any worse. Closing them down might have been considered an educational advancement.

Since schools are a politically dangerous area in which to openly meddle, Daley had maintained the pose of not being directly involved in their management. That was the job of the school board. But he appointed the members of the school board, and they elected their president and vice-president. The two offices were filled by President Frank Whiston, a politically connected real estate man-

agement company president, and Thomas Murray, boss
of the Electricians' Union. Both were white, old, conservative, and loyal to Daley and his beliefs. Daley's pose
of noninvolvement in the schools was enhanced by the
fact that a citizens' advisory committee, made up of
leaders of civic organizations, screened candidates and
made recommendations before he appointed them. Since
he had some of his men on the citizens' board, however,
they usually recommended people he could trust. But
when the schools deteriorated to the point of crisis, the
citizens' committee took the bold step of recommending
that Murray and Whiston be dropped when their terms
expired. One of Daley's friends on the committee said:
"I warned them not to do that, not to flaunt their recommendations publicly that way. I told them if they just left
it up to him, and quietly let him know how they felt, that
maybe, just maybe, he might drop those two. But they
didn't listen to me, and they made their recommendations
public, so he did just what I expected. He turned right
around and reappointed them. He's not letting anybody
tell him what to do."

One by one, and sometimes several at a time, he had
crushed the people who rose up during the postconven-
tion years of discontent. The shouts of the community
groups that had fought his urban renewal policies became
nothing more than a frustrated whisper, as the bulldozers
went on, sweeping away old but often usable housing and
leaving behind nothing but empty land that someday
would be grabbed by the big real estate operators. In his
time, urban renewal had wiped out housing for almost
thirty thousand families, most of it of the low-rent variety.
Urban renewal had replaced it with only eleven thousand
units, most of it of the high-rise, high-rent variety. The
blacks and the poor were still being used as chess pieces
by the real estate men, who worked hand-in-pocket with
City Hall.
On the drawing boards in 1970 was the next big renewal target—a huge piece of the near Northwest Side,
twenty-six hundred acres of homes, apartments, and
stores, most of it holding low-income people. It would be
bulldozed, and if the pattern was followed, would be re-

placed by middle- and high-income housing only. Billions in profits, and the poor would pack and push on. The community was supposed to decide what urban renewal would do to them by electing their representatives to pass all plans. But that problem had been taken care of by City Hall, which loaded up the Community Conservation Board with its puppets.

"People don't understand what we're after, or what we're talking about," said an urban renewal official. "This is fortunate, because if they did, we'd all have to run for cover."

The blacks on his Police Department had tried to rebel. They formed an Afro-American police association, pushing for a fair break in promotions, for less brutality against their people, and an end to the Irish domination of the department. Their leader, Renault Robinson, who always had an excellent record, suddenly was hit with suspension after suspension. He was followed, harassed, arrested. When he tried to organize a black ghetto parade on St. Patrick's Day, he was ordered to work and assigned to direct traffic for Daley's State Street parade. The blacks' rebellion became, at best, dormant.

On his sixty-eighth birthday, Daley could expect to hear from all of his old friends, the men who had helped him and whom he had rewarded. He had put them in their places, and they were pleased. Fire Commissioner Quinn would always be at a birthday party. Now past retirement age, he has remained on the job. "I think he keeps Quinn around," said Ald. Seymour Simon, "because Quinn always reminds him if he forgets to zip up his pants when he comes out of the bathroom."

He'd surely hear from Morgan Murphy, the boyhood friend who had become chairman of the executive committee at Commonwealth Edison. He had taken good care of Morgan, Jr., a hulking, unimaginative, sad-eyed young man who had been rammed down the throats of black voters as their representative in Congress. One of Murphy's nephews had become a judge while in his thirties, and remained on the bench even after being caught going out at night to sign bonds for crooks represented by lawyer friends. Another Murphy nephew shot up through police ranks to captain. But most of all, Daley helped Morgan's company. Commonwealth Edison was the biggest single air polluter in Chicago, its power plants belching soft-coal smoke that accounted for one-third of the pollution. When antipollution groups began pushing, the City Council passed a tougher law, with specific deadlines for the reduction of soft coal. But when Commonwealth Edison said it couldn't find hard coal, City Hall casually waived the deadlines. Daley didn't have to worry about protests from the city's official Air Pollution Control Appeal Board: his nephew was the chairman, and the members included the manager of a chemical company that was a big polluter, the brother of an executive of a steel company, another big polluter, and good old "Doc" O'Connell, who didn't think pollution was a serious problem.

Tom Keane is usually at the party for his slice of cake, if he is not somewhere else slicing up a pie. In the basement of Keane's seventeen-room, art-filled mansion hangs an old newspaper cartoon. "Look at it," says Keane. "It's from the *Tribune* in 1955, and it's the original. Don Maxwell got it for me." Maxwell is the ultra-conservative former publisher of the *Tribune*. "We're good friends you know," Keane says. The cartoon portrays Daley as a grinning wind-up doll, clutching a sign that says "Give Chicago leadership." Holding the oversized doll-crank are caricatures of John D'Arco, the Syndicate's political representative, William Dawson, the black boss, Joe Gill, the party ancient, Artie Elrod, the Twenty-fourth Ward boss, Paddy Bauler, a boisterous ward boss and saloon keeper, and Keane himself, all smiling evilly. "We were going to dominate him," Keane says. "That's what everybody was saying then. Every time Daley comes over here, he looks at that thing and he laughs."

The young ones always pay their respects, the Ray Simons and Matt Danahers and Dave Stahls, all waiting and wondering which of them will someday sit in his chair. It was likely on his sixty-eighth birthday that they would have a long wait. "He's got a compulsion about being mayor," says one of his cronies. "He couldn't live without it. If he got out, it would be a terrible traumatic shock for him. He used to be able to get away for two-week vacations, fish, play golf, relax. Now the only place he can breathe is on the fifth floor of City Hall. He's got a compulsion for work. He can't quit. It's almost a sickness. If he can, he's going to hold onto it until he is dead. I'm sure he wants to die in office."

And why not? He had worked all those years to get it, and it was his, the Machine, the city, and nobody could stare him down. Even Cardinal John Cody, the head of the Chicago archdiocese, the biggest in the nation, was nervous in his presence and stayed clear of him. Others had made it to the top, as he had, but something always did them in. Sometimes it was greed. After all his years up there, nobody could even say he ever took a nickel. Nobody would ever know. The financial affairs of presidents became an open book, as with Lyndon B. Johnson's radio dealings. Other mayors had been so obvious that it was no surprise when Ed Kelly died and left more than a million in small bills in a safe deposit box. But Daley, for all anyone knew, could be flat broke or secretly wealthy. Besides the small house on Lowe, there was only the sprawling summer home on the beach in Michigan, and that had been picked up at a bargain —forty thousand dollars. He didn't drink, he was faithful to Sis, and even his kids stayed out of trouble. He could look any man in the eye. Or at least he should have been able to.

It should have been a good sixty-eighth birthday party, and City Hall should have been a happy place, but it wasn't to be. Keeping everybody in their proper place does have a price. And that day a federal grand jury was making public a report that showed how high the price could be.

The report dealt with a police raid that had occurred in December 1969 on a West Side flat occupied by several Black Panther party leaders. The raid had been conducted by the office of State's Attorney Edward Hanrahan, the most ambitious of Daley's protégés. Hanrahan, a vile-tempered, intense man, had risen through the party routine and had become the Machine's loudest advocate of law and order. In his first big job as U.S. attorney for northern Illinois he grabbed headlines in a series of prosecutions of Mafia gangsters, although most of the planning and work was done by a special unit from Washington. Hanrahan had, in fact, been considered something of a blunderer by his Washington superiors, but those distinctions were lost on the voters, and in 1968 he was Daley's choice to retain the important state's attorney's office for the Machine in the disastrous year for the Democrats.

Daley liked Hanrahan because he, more than any other young prospect in the party, reflected Daley's social attitudes. Despite being a Harvard law graduate, Hanrahan ranted about law and order in the same terms as a gnarled desk sergeant. His answer to most social problems boiled down to locking people up for the maximum sentence. Like Daley, he hated the press and feuded constantly with reporters. Like Daley, he had an explosive temper, and even a reputation as a barroom brawler. Once, while U.S. attorney, he went out after a Democratic state convention in Chicago and, hours later, turned up at a suburban hospital with a battered face. Because of his appearance, he didn't show up in his office for almost a week.

It wasn't surprising, then, that Hanrahan, after the 1968 elections, declared war on the young black street gangs and on the Black Panther party. The black gangs frightened Daley, and it wasn't because they shot at each other, or because some of them had committed murders in their membership drives and wars over territories. One of the gangs, the Black P. Stone Nation, had grown to a loose-knit membership of several thousand and was beginning to show signs of political and economic awareness and the use of such power. Black politicians were currying its favor, and private social agencies were making efforts to channel it into legitimate business activities. Daley had seen the same thing happen before. He recalled Regan's Colts, the Irish thieves and street fighters who became the most potent political force in neighboring Canaryville, and his own neighborhood's Hamburgs, who got their start the same brawling way before turning to politics and eventually launching his career. There lay the danger of the black gangs. Blacks had been killing each other for years without inspiring any great concern in City Hall.

But these young toughs could be dictating who their aldermen would be if he didn't stop them. And the Black
Panthers, a more sophisticated though smaller group, was
even more dangerous. They had set up a free-food program in the ghetto and had opened a health clinic that was
superior to those of his own health department.

The Police Department had already been applying
constant pressure when Hanrahan came charging in with
his personal war. The police Gang Intelligence Unit was,
in fact, bigger than the unit assigned to crime syndicate
activities. But Hanrahan created a special unit of his own
for the same purpose.

It was this unit, made up of fourteen of the one hundred
Chicago policemen assigned to Hanrahan's staff, that
went to the Panther flat at 4 A.M. on December 4, 1969,
with a search warrant, supposedly looking for a cache of
unregistered guns. When the raid was over, they had the
guns, and two Panther leaders were dead: Fred Hampton,
the Chicago chairman, who had been reared in the black
middle class area of Maywood, one of the few integrated
suburbs; and Mark Clark, a downstate Panther leader.
Four other Panthers had been wounded.

Hanrahan that morning said it was a miracle that his
men had escaped unharmed, so vicious was the hail of
gunfire that answered their knock on the door to the slum
apartment. His men, in telling their story of the raid,
agreed. Even before the bodies were toe-tagged at the
morgue, the police raiders told in great detail of Panther
bullets ripping through doors at them, of shotgun blasts
from bedrooms, and of policemen leaping out of the way
of hunting-rifle slugs. They said they repeatedly pleaded
with the Panthers to surrender, but each plea was answered by bullets, which forced them to retaliate.

Their story dominated the papers and television for
three days, with the familiar charges by surviving Panthers
that the police had murdered without provocation, which
nobody believed. But then a couple of reporters went
through the flat, which had been opened to the black community by the Panthers, found obvious evidence that no
gun battle had occurred, and reported it. It was clear that
Hanrahan's men had done virtually all of the shooting.
The bullet holes were in the interior of the flat, where the

Panthers had been. The areas near the doors, the doors themselves, and the walls opposite the Panther bedrooms were virtually unmarked. At most, there was evidence of one Panther bullet having been fired, while dozens of police bullet holes tore through the thin walls of the bedrooms, killing Hampton in his bed.

When the story of the contradictions hit the papers, Hanrahan reacted wildly, hysterically labeling the reporters liars, ordering his men to appear on television to reenact the gun battle in a studio mock-up of the apartment, and persuaded the willing *Chicago Tribune* to print a story full of factual errors, outright lies, distortions, and pictures of nail holes that were described as Panther bullet holes.

But pressure from even the most moderate blacks was mounting for an investigation, and a federal grand jury was convened to look into the case. President Nixon's Justice Department saw no reason to shield Daley from embarrassment. And despite the refusal of the distrustful surviving Panthers to testify, the grand jury investigation was held, based primarily on material gathered by the FBI.

So on Daley's birthday, of all days, the report was made public and it was damning. It found that there had been no gun battle of the kind described by Hanrahan's men. Only one spent bullet could be traced to the Panthers, and eighty to one hundred to the police. The police had apparently sprayed the flat with shotgun, pistol, and machine-gun fire, with little provocation.

Since there had been no gun battle, it followed that Hanrahan's men had been lying. This, too, was a grand jury finding. Beyond lies to the press, there had been deliberate misrepresentation of physical evidence. The Chicago Police crime laboratory had lied about its ballistic tests. A laboratory functionary admitted this to the grand jury, saying he had feared losing his job if he didn't fake evidence. The grand jury found, too, that the police Internal Investigations Division had intentionally whitewashed its investigation of police conduct during the raid.

Daley, warned in advance that the report was coming, tried to blunt its impact by shuffling around some of the top police brass in the sections that were being criticized.

In human terms, the report should have meant a scandal far more serious than the 1960 Summerdale affair. Then property had been stolen. This time people had been slaughtered, and the slaughter clumsily covered up by officials. Daley knew, from experience, what the next steps would be. A special county prosecutor would have to be appointed by the court to investigate Hanrahan's men. If any of the policemen were indicted and convicted, Daley would philosophize, as he always had in matters of public misconduct by one of his people: "Even the Lord had skeptical members of his party. One betrayed him, one denied him, and one doubted him. And so we have to take human nature for what it is." The way Daley always put it, the Disciples were members of a political party.

Beyond that ritual dance, no further steps would have to be taken. A genuine reorganization of the Police Department wouldn't be necessary, as it had been in 1960, because the killing of Black Panthers and the routine brutality toward blacks was not offensive to most of the city's white voters. As for the indignation of blacks, word would be leaked to the press that Hanrahan was through politically, that when his term ran out in three years, he would be dumped. When the time came, it might not be necessary, memories being short in politics. But if it had to be done, Hanrahan could be given a judgeship as a token reward for party service and, of greater importance, for absorbing the brunt of criticism, which allowed Daley to stand aside, as almost a bystander, and cluck that he was shocked by it all.

The limousine came that morning to take him to City Hall, but he sent it away. Reporters were told that he would spend the day at home with family and a few friends. The traditional birthday party was canceled. On his sixty-eighth birthday, in the city he had ruled for so long, he couldn't go to his own office because there would be questions for which he had no ready answers. The timing of the report seemed like a cruel act of fate. But it wasn't. As with most other things that happened in his city, the timing of the report had been arranged by him. It gave him an excuse to stay home that day, and nobody could say he was hiding. In his Chicago, even a man's birthday could be put to a political use. "Chicago ain't ready for reform yet," Alderman Bauler said when Daley was elected in 1955. And in 1970, ready or not, it wasn't getting any.

Epilogue

On April 6, 1971, Daley was elected to his fifth term as mayor. His opponent, Richard Friedman, a liberal Democrat, tried to form a coalition of liberals, independents, disgruntled blacks, and ran under the Republican label. The spirit of Daley's final campaign was best stated by Ald. Claude Holman, a South Side boss, who said:

"We must win so big, so overwhelmingly, so abundantly, that never again will that array of so-called phony independents join up with the opposition or dare challenge the big heart and mind and courage of our leader. We must win coming down the stretch like a thundering herd."

The day after the election, somebody else said: "This proves that if you put together a coalition of independents, blacks, liberals, and Republicans, there is no way Daley can keep you from getting twenty-nine percent of the vote."

Daley received slightly more than seventy percent of the vote and carried forty-eight of the city's fifty wards, despite Friedman's having waged the most spirited, imaginative campaign of any of Daley's five opponents. Daley also maintained full control of his City Council.

The lopsided victory left Daley in a position to eventually choose his successor, a role a narrow victory would have denied him. And once again he was going to be the man to see at the Democratic Convention.

The morning after election, he met the press in City Hall. He was asked if he had heard from any of the

Presidential hopefuls. The reporters rattled off the names Edward Kennedy, George McGovern, Hubert Humphrey, Edmund Muskie.

"Have any of them telephoned with congratulations?" he was asked.

Daley smiled. "All of them did."

Index

Index

219